A PRIMER FOR DEVELOPMENTAL METHODOLOGY

BY *Douglas Friedrich*, CENTRAL MICHIGAN UNIVERSITY

BURGESS PUBLISHING COMPANY • MINNEAPOLIS, MINN.

Copyright © 1972 by Burgess Publishing Company
Printed in the United States of America
Library of Congress Catalog Card Number 72-87182
SBN 8087-0621-7

All rights reserved. No part of this book may be reproduced in any form whatsoever, by photograph or mimeograph or by any other means, by broadcast or transmission, by translation into any kind of language, nor by recording electronically or otherwise, without permission in writing from the publisher, except by a reviewer, who may quote brief passages in critical articles and reviews.

1 2 3 4 5 6 7 8 9 0

PREFACE

Quite simply, this Primer on development models and methods is based on my frustrations in undergraduate and graduate school. Although I found the field of development (e.g., embryology; child and adolescent psychology) appealing, the typical misuse of theory, use of sloppy theory, and lack of relevant data collection and analyzing techniques in the various fields relating to development were disturbing. Students of development, past and present, find many interesting ideas that stimulate curiosity of life in general and behavioral change in particular. This stimulation is certainly not peculiar to students. Contemporary texts and journals (general, professional) in the behavioral sciences are emphasizing the need to apply developmental ideas to numerous individual and social problems. Unfortunately, the developmental ideas are not well delineated, nor are such hypotheses based on sound methodology or models. My contention is that developmental hypotheses based on poor methods of data collection and data organization hinder the student and professional in attempting to solve the multitude of problems facing society.

It is fair to acknowledge that useful developmental models (fact-organization) and methodology (fact-finding) are presently available. Such developmental models and methods are based, for the most part, on the efforts of a relatively small group of participants at the *West Virginia Life-Span Conferences.* Fortunately, the influence of the *Conference* is rapidly growing through such avenues as (a) journal articles and book chapters, for professional consumption, and (b) graduate and undergraduate classroom teaching for student consumption. It is fair to state that the "sophisticated" developmental models and methods are implemented by relatively few professionals. Further, very few undergraduate and graduate students have an elementary knowledge of useful developmental models and methods. Fortunately, the contemporary developmental data gathering and organizing techniques are not difficult to assimilate, since the basis of the achievements are classical developmental models and methods. The purpose of this Primer is to introduce students of behavioral change to model and methodological advancements in the area of development.

This Primer should also prove useful to students interested in the classic experimental approach to describing and/or explaining behavior. The experimental approach, though emphasizing appropriate models and methods, deals only minimally with such developmental variables as race, sex, age, socioeconomic status, and culture. If experimentalists are to effectively deal with developmental issues (and contemporary journal articles indicate such participation), they must become aware of appropriate developmental models and methodology for reliable and valid principles. My point is that developmental issues and problems require developmental-specific models and methodology.

Although this Primer is the result of my concern for developmental-specific models and methods, numerous individuals contributed in one way or another to its completion. Dr. Don C. Charles (Iowa State University) introduced me to the importance of employing a developmental framework in attempting to deal with individual and group behavioral issues. He also introduced me to the problems of model building and methodology in development. Dr. William F. Hawkins (Central Michigan University), with his continual encouragement, increased my motivation to complete the Primer. Ms. Theresa Kenney did more than type the manuscript. Her ability to make sense out of nonsense is unbelievable. Finally, I thank my wife, Connie, for "babying" me throughout this, and other, projects. A fellow professional deserves a better fate.

June, 1972   Douglas Friedrich

CONTENTS

Preface	iii
Contents	v
Introduction to Developmental Methodology	1
Basic Elements of Development	11
Classical Developmental Designs	19
Developmental Design Components	40
Multivariate Data Collection Designs: Sequential Strategies	45
Multivariate Data Collection Designs: Dependent Variables	77
Concluding Comments	107
References	109
Subject Index	119
Name Index	121

INTRODUCTION TO DEVELOPMENTAL METHODOLOGY

IN THE PAST FEW years, two broad areas directly related to behavioral change have been reemphasized: *developmental psychology* and *research methodology*. This Primer is based on an integration of these areas. There are several obvious reasons for an introduction to the integration of developmental principles and research methodology. First, in this era of applied research, a concern for methodology cannot be left only to classic experimental or natural science programs. That is, students of human behavior interested in such applied areas as community relations, social problems, mental health, or clinical practice *must* become *at least* acquainted with methods of collecting, analyzing, summarizing, and integrating data. As is the case of *Head Start,* remedial programs to combat social problems have failed miserably without the benefits of applied methodological principles and model delineation. Social ills such as racism, cultural deprivation, mental illness, crime, and drug usage cannot be cured simply by *concerned* individuals. All too frequently, attempts by *concerned* people to alleviate social problems result in frustration and waste (e.g., massive federal spending). It is argued here that humanistic remediation attempts *must* be based on sound facts about the particular social problem. A prerequisite to obtaining sound facts is an awareness of appropriate methods of data gathering, data analysis, data summarization, and data integration.

A second reason for introducing an integration of developmental principles and research methodology relates to disciplines of human behavior. No longer can any *specific* discipline of human behavior (basic or applied) deny the importance of a developmental framework in attempting to describe or explain human behavior. Although most behavioral models are static (nondevelopmental), there is much evidence available to support the assertion that developmental principles are basic to model-building in the behavioral sciences. A basic aspect of human behavior is that of *change over time.* Consequently, much classic research in the many areas of behavioral analysis has come under criticism because of a lack of consideration for developmental issues. More specifically, many behavioral theories are classified as static because of a lack of concern for such qualitative changes that are age-related, sex-related, culture-related, and species-related.

DIMENSIONS OF DEVELOPMENTAL MODELS

There are two types of changes implicit in developmental models: *qualitative* and *quantitative*. Qualitative change developmental models represent the labeling or characteristics summarization approach; i.e., associated or correlated organismic characteristics (overt behaviors) are incorporated as referents of a given level of organismic adaptation to the environment. Briefly, the qualitative approach deals with levels or stages of development and each stage or level is defined or delineated by specific behaviors. The quantitative change developmental approach investigates a specific referent or ability; e.g., language, memory, or perception—through periods of the life span. The emphasis on quantitative change and development has been discussed by Flavell and Wohlwill (1969). These developmentalists provide a rationale for the two types of developmental change: qualitatively-looking change and quantitatively-looking change. Qualitatively-looking changes are best illustrated by Bruner's *modes of representation* developmental theory *(inactive, iconic,* and *symbolic* stages) and Piaget's *stages of cognitive development (sensorimotor, preoperational, concrete operations,* and *formal operations)*. These modes and stages represent qualitatively-looking change within the organism; qualitative change is defined by specific behavioral referents. Quantitatively-looking changes refer to "changes in the operational efficiency, flexibility, mobility, and such like, of each of the specific referents for general levels of adaptation during all or part of the organism's developmental life" (Flavell and Wohlwill, 1969, p. 78). If the developmentalist is concerned with specific referents of general dependent variables, or general levels, the important question is whether qualitative or quantitative changes occur in these specific referents as the organism develops. It is important to note that quantitative change in specific referent does not include possible changes in the interdependent relationship of such referents; e.g., Bruner's (1964) hypothesis of an "orchestration" of referents into an integrated system. More specifically, changes in the interdependent relationship of specific referents is the major criterion for progression through stages of cognitive development. The best known example of the change in referent interrelationships criterion is Piaget's cognitive-developmental stage approach. Piaget proposes five criteria for progression through stages of cognitive development: (a) *hierarchization* (fixed order of progression through levels constituting a developmental sequence); (b) *integration* (processes of a given stage S_2 integrate those of the preceding stage S_1); (c) *consolidation* (a given stage S_2 must incorporate referents of the preceding stage S_1 and referents, or elementary forms of referents, of the successive stage S_3; (d) *structuring* (organization or "orchestration" of cognitive processes at a given stage characteristic of a particular level of functioning); and (e) *equilibration* (not characteristic of any given stage, but plays a role similar to consolidation over the entire developmental series) (Pinard and Laurendeau, 1969). It appears appropriate to discuss all of the above criteria in terms of the single criterion, changing interdependent referent relationships. Qualitative differences refer to changes in referent interrelationships; changes in specific referents are interpreted as due to quantitative change only.

Looft (1972) has recently examined contemporary theoretical approaches in the broad areas of socialization and personality. Since Looft's analysis is quite relevant to a life-span orientation, his dimensions for classifying developmental theoretical approaches are listed and discussed below:

DIMENSIONS ON WHICH DEVELOPMENTAL THEORIES VARY

1. *External vs. Internal Locus of the Developmental Dynamic*
2. *Qualitative vs. Quantitative Change*
3. *Closed vs. Open System*
4. *Continuous vs. Discontinuous Change*
5. *Reductionism vs. Emergence*
6. *Elementarism vs. Holism*
7. *Structure-Function vs. Antecedent-Consequent Analysis*
8. *Structural vs. Behavioral Change*
9. *Nature of Individual Differences*
10. *Status of Chronological Age*
11. *Directionality of Development*
12. *Universality vs. Relativity of Development*

Dimension 1 refers to the issue of whether development is based on changes *within the organism* or on *changes external to the organism.* Theories of the former orientation are referred to as organismic, those of the latter as mechanistic. Piaget's cognitive adaptation theory is usually classified as an organismic one; development is the result of an active organism processing information from the environment. Social learning and behavior modification orientations (both based on Skinnerian learning paradigms) are usually classified as mechanistic; change in the individual due to external stimulus manipulation.

Dimension 2 qualitative vs. quantitative change, was discussed in detail in the previous section. Briefly, qualitative change (e.g., Piagetian model) theories postulate stages or levels of development with uniqueness among stages, and quantitative change (behavior modification, learning) theories postulate cumulative effects of environmental manipulation on given overt behaviors.

Dimension 3 is closely related to the external-internal and qualitative-quantitative change dichotomies. Open system orientations view development as an "accumulation of skills, habits, and other behaviors in basically an additive, linear fashion." Human development is viewed as "essentially a panorama of more and more [development], or, perhaps, less and less [deterioration]" (Looft, 1972, p. 8). Closed systems are less optimistic, postulating organismic capabilities as essentially fixed-limited. Again, learning theories are examples of an open system and organismic (including behavior-genetic) theories are examples of a closed system. Gagné's (1968) cumulative learning model, an open system, emphasizes the more and more orientation; i.e., sophisticated capabilities of the individual based on simple habits stimulus-response chains. Piaget's theory clearly is an example of a closed system. His last, and most adaptive, cognitive stage (formal operation) is qualitatively different than the antecedent stage and is an end point in his developmental theory.

Dimension 4 (related to Dimension 2) categorizes theories according to pattern of behavioral change. Is development "categorized by steady, quantitative change [cumulative learning model], or is it a sequence of saltatory, qualitative changes [stage approach]" (Looft, p. 9)?

Dimension 5 is certainly related to the previous four. Reductionistic theories (e.g., Gagné's cumulative learning) postulate that every higher-order capability or skill may be reduced to its elementary or simple elements. A simple illustration of the reductionistic approach is Bijou's (1968) loosely defined postulate that complex behavioral patterns (language, personality) are primarily based on basic classical and instrumental conditioning paradigms. The opposite of reductionism is emergence; succeeding structures and capabilities of development are not reducible to preceding, simpler components. Organismic models, stressing qualitative differences among stages, fit nicely into the emergent category.

Dimension 6 (elementarism vs. holism) is related to the previous five dimensions.

> Into the mechanical model is incorporated the corollary principle of elementarism, which, in essence, asserts that the whole (man) can be assembled by piecing together its isolated parts. Stated in another way, the whole can be predicted from its parts. . . . In contrast, the holistic viewpoint insists that the organism possesses an organization that disallows a breaking-down-and-piecing-back-together analysis. Behavior is to be assessed in the context within which it is embedded; included, therefore, must be considerations of the individual at a multitude of levels and perspectives—physical status, goals, self-knowledge, environmental surround, and so forth" (Looft, pp. 11-12).

Dimension 7 may be defined in simple terms. Structure-function theories are concerned with specifying the functions, objectives, or general purpose of the individual and then postulating underlying associated psychological structures. Such theories are teleological and deterministic; there is inherent order to development and the phenomena of physiological life may be explained by mentalistic, purposive causes. Antecedent-consequent theorists are primarily interested in behavior and argue that "any given behavioral phenomenon can be interpreted as the consequence of a set of prior antecedents" (Looft, p. 12). Although antecedent-consequent theorists may deal with non-observables (intervening variables, mediating mechanisms), such constructs are defined by antecedent observables, consequent observables, or both.

Dimension 8 deals with the fundamental issue of just what are the changes inherent in the concept of development. The structural system deals with abstractions or derived variables, hypothesizing inferred changes in psychological structures underlying behavioral manifestations. The behavioral approach disregards inferred changes in non-observable organismic structures and deals only with behavior. Essentially, this dimension is exactly the same as the traditional controversy of *nothing but* (behavioral approach) and *something more* (structural approach).

Dimension 9 (individual differences) reflects two classification schemes.

Scheme A (Emmerich, 1968)
1. *Classical* theorists, (Piaget, Freud) argue for an invariant (constant) sequence of developmental stage progression. Individual differences are dealt with in terms of age norms (inter-individual variation) corresponding to stages. *Rate* of progression through stages identifies individual differences (fast, slow, average progression).
2. *Differential* theorists (Cattell, Guilford) depict individual differences in terms of an individual's location on trait or attribute dimensions (low, medium, high). This is typically a psychometric approach; individuals are tested on intelligence and personality tests and are compared with others on each subtest (trait, attribute).
3. *Ipsative* theorists are concerned with changes within the individual (intra-individual variation); changes in trait or attribute interrelationships over time or situations.

Scheme B (Van den Daele, 1969)
1. *Unitary* theorists postulate that individuals progress through stages or levels along a single developmental track. Individual differences can occur only in the *rate* of progression (similar to classical approach in Scheme A).
2. *Multiple* theorists suggest that individuals may progress (at different rates) along a number of developmental tracks (i.e., progression through multiple transformations of stages and substages). Multiple progression assumes various developmental alternatives or sequences (alternative developmental paths).
3. *Simple* developmental models postulate that an individual can occupy only one developmental stage or level at a given point in time. Simple models attempt to find age-related order and, necessarily, deal with inter-individual rather than intra-individual variation. Piaget's cognitive adapta-

tion model, postulating hierarchical transformation and successive stages, is a simple developmental model.

4. *Cumulative* developmental models postulate more than one developmental level or structure, and an individual may operate at various levels or structures at a given point in time. Cumulative theorists argue for within-individual alternatives, and an individual may function at various levels of cognitive complexity at a given period in time.

Van den Daele's four properties of developmental models are postulated within a two (unitary-multiple) by two (simple-cumulative) classification matrix. Van den Daele provides the following developmental model examples represented by the matrix:

SIMPLE, UNITARY PROGRESSION

The simple, unitary progression posits an invariant sequence of particular organizations or characteristics, *b* always follows *a*, and *c* always follows *b*: a b c. . . . Although the simple, unitary model serves as the general model for the preponderance of developmental analyses, the model excludes alternative progressions and restricts alternative organizations. The only meaning which may be imputed to individual differences is a faster or slower rate of progression through stages (Emmerich, 1966; Kessen, 1966). . . .

The model is exemplified by Piaget's cognitive stages. His criteria of hierarchical transformation stress the articulation of successive stages such that, *a b c* . . ., or, at least, *a* R *b*, *b* R *c*. . . . These requirements do not ipso facto determine a unitary progression, but with the representation of cognition as a logically hierarchized, group structure, coherent alternative structures are much restricted, if not eliminated.

SIMPLE, MULTIPLE PROGRESSION

The simple, multiple progression implies alternative developmental sequences of particular organizations. Any stage or stages may be followed by any number of alternative stages, although only one stage may belong to one person at one time. The simple, multiple model is associated with analyses concerned with the development of general individual differences, including interpersonal orientation, behavioral style, and personality. The model is implicit in physiological and embryological studies of developmental anomaly (Bonner, 1963; Scott, 1962; Sinnott, Dunn, and Dobzhansky, 1958).

The simple, multiple progression is exemplified by Erikson's (1963) "binary fission" model of ego development. Persons are confronted by mutually exclusive alternatives at each stage, the choice of one rather than the other affecting all subsequent choices. The movement from stage to stage eventuates in individual as well as developmental differences.

CUMULATIVE, UNITARY PROGRESSION

The cumulative, unitary progression presumes the maintenance of some earlier and later stages of a single sequence: a ab abc . . . . The model implies one "proper" path, but accommodates to a within-person hierarchy of alternative structures derived from developmentally more primitive modes of response. . . .

The six stages of moral development described by Kohlberg (1963) occur in a single invariant sequence. Although Kohlberg argues that a later stage may displace an earlier stage, his results appear consistent with a cumulative model. Persons implement alternative, developmentally related rationales clustered about a model stage to justify moral choice. Persons retain some earlier with later orientations, but not all previous orientations (Kohlberg, 1963, p. 17).

CUMULATIVE, MULTIPLE PROGRESSION

The cumulative, multiple progression implies the coexistence of earlier and later stages along with the option of developmentally alternative characteristics or organizations, accommodating to between- as well as within-person differences. . . .

Freud (1962), discussing some of the premises of psychoanalytic theory, wrote, "in mental life nothing which has once been formed can perish—. . . everything is somehow preserved [p. 16]." Moreover, what is preserved is maintained alongside the "transformed version [p. 15]." These transformations, as well as the original experience, are contingent upon genetic-environmental factors which dictate discrete modes of symbolic and drive transformation (Freud, 1933, pp. 153-185). Hence, the implicit psychoanalytic model may be construed as cumulative (the preservation of earlier structures) and multiple (discrete modes of symbolic transformation) [pp. 307-308].

Dimension 10, chronological age, is discussed in detail in a later section of the Primer. Briefly, the dichotomy here is that some developmental camps utilize age as a marker for stage or level progression (organismic, qualitative change theories), and other camps completely reject the use of age as a marker and/or attempts to explain age differences (mechanistic, quantitative change theories). Thus, qualitative change, organismic theorists utilize age differences as boundary markers for stages of development. Mechanistic, quantitative change theorists are concerned only with behavior and *change in behavior;* age has no utility in such a system of analysis.

Dimension 11 categorizes developmental models into (a) those advocating progression, increasing complexity, and expansion, and (b) those advocating progression and regression. Point *a* represents the traditional view of the concept of development and is illustrated by organismic models. Point *b*, advocated by most personality theorists, states that individuals can, and often do, revert back to earlier, more elementary (primitive) forms of dealing with the environment. In fact, the concepts of fixation and regression are primary in most developmental theories of personality (e.g., Freud, Cameron, Erikson).

Finally, *Dimension 12* (universality vs. relativity) deals with the issue of general or specific (unique) development or behavioral change. Are there principles of development that are universal, i.e., "common to all biologically intact human beings" (Looft, p. 25)? Again, organismic models usually postulate that underlying structures of behavioral change are universal. Since most organismic models recognize the importance of genetic programming, the concept of invariant genetic programs for a given species would also support the notion of universality of development. Proponents of reactive, quantitative models would argue that development is unique for each individual. That is, each individual develops in relatively unique situations (environmental manipulations). Where similarities in behavior exist among individuals, the relativist would argue that similar environmental factors were operating. Likewise differences among individuals are explained by the differences in environmental conditions impinging on the various organisms.

Looft's delineation of dimensions on which developmental theories vary is crucial to the scope of this Primer. It is important for the student to recognize that developmental theories do differ on numerous dimensions. Developmental models and methods, which are the main issues in this Primer, reflect, in part, the various theoretical orientations of developmentalists. Important concerns in the Primer deal with integrating discrepant developmental models and methods into a multidimensional developmental model with alternative research methodologies.

"LAWS" OF BEHAVIORAL CHANGE

The present concern in professional circles for developmental analyses is based on the rather recent realization that descriptive or normative developmental research is an essential first step for explanation and/or prediction of human behavior. In this regard, it is interesting and informative to review contemporary articles in journals concerned with behavioral change—education, psychology, sociology, etc.—and find the *expressed* concern for reliable developmental trends. Unfortunately, much behavioral research, based on static, fixed model building, confounds treatment (independent variable) effects with organismic (dependent variable) effects. A more general formulation of much behavioral research is that such research avoids the issues raised by qualitative and quantitative developmental models. In fact, most students of human structure and process incorporate the following static psychological "laws" into their concepts (Berlyne, 1966; Spence, 1944):

1. *S-R Laws:* Expressing response variables as functions of stimulus variables; relationship between a given stimulus and a given response. As discussed in introductory psychology texts, there are numerous *S-R* theorists of behavior—Hull, Guthrie, Mowrer, Skinner. Reduced to the basic formula, *S-R* approaches treat each response in relation to a given stimulus. A

specific stimulus-response pairing makes possible the use of probability statements that a particular response will occur given a particular stimulus.

2. *S-S Laws:* Expressing correlations between response variables; relationship between or among various behaviors. *S-S* approaches fall within the broad field of psychometrics. This field is concerned with sequences or clusters of responses that occur together. Reduced to elementary terms, the *S-S* approach deals with the relationship among given responses. Standardized IQ and personality tests are examples of tools employed within psychometrics to assess correlations or relationships among responses.

3. *S-I Laws:* Enabling values of intervening concepts[1] (hypothetical conditions within the organism) to be deduced from values of stimulus variables; relationship between stimulus and "hypothetical" internal state of the organism. Hull, in his general behavior theory, attempted to employ the intervening variable, i.e., its meaning is totally defined by stimulus and response referents. With *S-I* laws, the intervening concept is defined by *stimulus* referents.

4. *I-R Laws:* Enabling values of intervening concepts to be deduced from values of response variables; relationship between response and "hypothetical" internal state of the organism. With *I-R* laws, the intervening concept is defined by *response* referents.

5. *SI-R Laws:* Expressing response variables as functions of specific stimulus and general organismic variables; relationship among stimulus, organismic, and response variables. The important distinction in *SI-R* approaches is a recognition of organismic characteristics such as species differences and sex differences.

Berlyne (1966), recognizing the importance of descriptive developmental research, suggests two additional laws:

6. *A-R Laws:* Expressing the incidence of various behaviors at various ages; relationship among responses or behaviors at different ages. The *A-R* approach, although extremely general, is developmental in nature.

---

1. There are two types of intervening constructs (Marx, 1963): intervening variables and hypothetical constructs. Intervening variables are summary devices and are *completely* defined by specific stimulus and/or response referents. Hypothetical constructs imply some physiological (internal) mechanism; such constructs imply *more* (surplus meaning) than the meaning provided by defined stimulus and/or response referents.

7. *SA-R Laws:* Expressing response variables as functions of specific stimulus and specific organismic—age-related—variables; relationship among specific stimulus, age, and response variables. This approach is simply an integration of the *A-R* and *S-R* approaches.

It is noted again that the above "laws" are basic to descriptive and/or explanatory attempts in the behavioral sciences. As will be discussed in the *"Multiple developmental model components* section, more specific psychological "laws" or dimensions than the seven listed above must be delineated for adequate behavioral model building. The important point to remember concerning psychological "laws" and principles of development is that although many theorists and researchers stress the importance of including a developmental framework within behavioral models, their theories and research usually indicate confounded organismic variable effects. That is, many behavioral theories avoid behavioral dimensions that reflect developmental principles—age, sex, culture, race, species, etc. Learning theories, for example, have been criticized for not delineating or unconfounding organismic effects within behavioral models. In fact, learning theorists assume a confounded organismic effect; i.e., much research on infrahumans is extrapolated to human behavior and species differences are minimized. As will be discussed below, a few contemporary developmental-learning theorists have given minimal attention to developmental principles within learning models. The practice of giving lip-service to a developmental framework, while avoiding issues of developmental principles, results in static behavioral models. Of course, it is one thing to accept a developmental framework in theory building and practical work, and quite another to understand the essentials of developmental methodology.

This Primer is concerned with the lack of sophistication for developmental methodology indicated by many researchers, practitioners, and students in various aspects of behavioral change. Unfortunately, only a few individuals concerned with human behavioral change are familiar with acceptable developmental designs, and even fewer individuals apply these designs in research, theory building, or practice. A common criticism made by academicians, and directed toward students, concerns the creative attempts of the latter in educational and social issues. Specifically, it has been noted that students often attack complex problems without the benefit of appropriate methodological principles and/or organization of facts and concepts. In recent years, the academicians have been similarly attacked. Of particular concern here is that students (in and out of school) interested in human behavior have not employed appropriate developmental models utilizing acceptable research methodology and applications. This Primer is based on the assumption that competency in the complex field of development requires a working knowledge of data collection (fact-finding) and organizational (fact-organization) methods.

BASIC ELEMENTS OF DEVELOPMENT

DEVELOPMENT MAY BE broadly defined as dealing with change over *time.* It has been recognized (Bijou, 1968; Friedrich, 1971) that time itself is not a relevant *causal* variable. Any system of behavior that employs time as a causal variable can only describe behavioral change as a function of an unspecified union of necessary variables—physical, psychological, and social. In the field of memory research, McGeoch's (1932) classic attack on Thorndike's Law of Disuse was an early critique of the time dimension. McGeoch pointed out that time itself does not cause anything; rather, events happen in time. Time does, however, provide a dimension in which critical and analyzable variables can be compared; it makes possible the study of behavioral change. Students of behavioral change are interested in organismic processes and structures which take place over time, not in time per se.

ELEMENTARY POINTS FOR STUDENTS OF DEVELOPMENT

Before reviewing experimental and quasi-experimental designs for behavioral change over time, it is necessary to comment on the expanding branch of behavioral science labeled "developmental." It is extremely unfortunate that both students and professionals interested in developmental aspects of behavior do not have an elementary knowledge of what development is all about. Because of this sad state the following points should not be passed over lightly; rather, the points reflect the confusion in the field of development.

1. Development *is not* restricted to any single period of the life span. There is no such thing as a developmental-child or developmental-adolescent specialist. In other words, a developmentalist *is not* a child specialist; he *is not* an adolescent specialist. He is a developmentalist—supposedly a specialist in physical and psychological change throughout the life span.
2. The discipline of development, at least as viewed in this Primer, is not a "fun-and-games" area. Development is not just a description of how kids behave in school. A consistent gripe from students in education, and concerning developmental courses, is that such courses deal too much with genetics, prenatal development, and physical change. The question often asked is: "Why do we have to know about that junk; what does it have to do with how kids perform in school?" The answer which should be given is: "The stuff you call junk refers to critical dimensions that relate to how kids do in school, or in a more global way, dimensions relating to behavioral change."

3. Development deals with organismic structure and function, and change in structure and function. The ability of any organism (human or infrahuman) to adapt to its environment reflects the basic structure (systems) and processes (functions) of that organism. Development *is not* restricted to personality development or intellectual development or physical development. Development deals with the organism's ability to adapt to its environment.
4. As specialists in a basic science, developmentalists need to understand and apply appropriate methods of fact investigation—data collection, analysis, summarization, and model building. Unfortunately, students are particulary upset when it comes to studying research design and statistics. The most frequently asked question concerning developmental methodology is: "What is the significance of learning about methods of inquiry in courses dealing with child (or adolescent) psychology?" As was pointed out earlier, child (or adolescent) psychology is not synonymous with developmental psychology. Further, in a complex discipline such as development, a basic understanding of fact-finding and fact-organization methods is a prerequisite of competency. Unfortunately, many individuals never pass from their student roll of "garbage collector." That is, many students insist on writing down everything an instructor says and then regurgitate it back on an exam. Many students also memorize (not assimilate!) information from texts. A very important result of such practices is that some students believe most everything (and anything) they read in textbooks or journals. Why do students of behavior *assume* a researcher has employed appropriate methods in attempting to solve specific problems? It is extremely important to remember that professionals—researchers, authors, teachers—make mistakes, often crucial mistakes. One means of assessing the competency of researchers, authors, and teachers is to subject their conclusions to critical methodogical review. This is possible only if the student has a basic understanding of methodological issues.
5. Development is not only a psychological concern; i.e., it is not restricted to developmental psychology. It should be obvious that much of our knowledge of development stems from such diverse areas as: genetics, physiology, history-anthropology, sociology, medicine, embryology, and linguistics. Development is truly a bastardized science, consisting of many specific disciplines.

Developmentalists cannot supply all the answers to developmental-related questions. In fact, the area of development includes many confusing issues. The most important of these issues are: (a) poor or inappropriate methodology; (b) restricted developmental models; and (c) restricted period or stage approaches. All three of these issues will be dealt with in detail in the Primer.

DEVELOPMENTAL DESIGN COMPONENTS

Subjecting development to a philosophy of science analysis, Nagel (1957) pointed out that the construct is one with protean meanings—sometimes employed to connote a process (description), sometimes the product of a process (eulogistic label). Following Nagel, the developmental construct incorporates a minimum of two components: "(a) the notion of a system [animal, machine, social] possessing a definite structure [physiological states, 'hardware,' institutions]; and (b) the notion of a sequential set of changes in the system, yielding relatively permanent but novel increments not only in its structure but in its modes of operation as well" (p. 17). Examples of Nagel's two developmental components are presented in Table 1.

Within the animal system, easily detectable structures are the respiratory, digestive, and visual subsystems. Since these structures follow maturational principles, it is easy to detect ongoing changes. For example, as the child matures, his lungs increase in size, mass, and volume. Also within the animal system, there are hypothesized, not-so-easy-to-detect structures. Examples of such structures include the memory, perceptual, and general cognitive subsystems. Again, such subsystems are abstractions, e.g., we cannot visually detect the memory subsystem. We can, however, make inferences about such subsystems through logical analyses. Abstract subsystems or structures lead to theories and model building. As will be presented in a later section of the Primer, developmental model building is an integral part of predicting or explaining behavioral change.

Most students of behavioral change accept the above developmental construct components, i.e., system-structure and change. Concerning the animal system, however, Riegel (1968) reports a major dilemma: "In spite of all the records collected, developmental scientists have not provided an answer to the question of why organisms grow and age" (pp. 5-6). Although most developmentalists accept the notions of system and change within the developmental construct, specific factors of development are difficult to delineate. The question of concern here is: "What specific events (inside and outside the organism) contribute to change in structure and process?"

In a recent review, Fowler (1970) noted that the *interactionist* theory is the most general prevailing conceptualization of the development of both mental and physical phenotypes.[2] That is, phenotypic development is regarded as a "joint product of the cumulative interaction of biological [including genetic] and environmental forces" (p. 141). This view of development rejects the dominance long ascribed to either genetic or environmental factors alone. It is

---

2. Phenotype refers to the observable characteristics of an organism; i.e., phenotype = observable organismic dependent variable.

TABLE 1

DEVELOPMENTAL CONSTRUCT COMPONENTS OF SYSTEM AND CHANGE

System	Structure	Change
Animal	Physiological states	Ontogenesis
Machine	"Hardware"	Technological advance
Social	Institutions	Organizational change

now generally recognized that neither environmental nor genetic factors alone can completely account for any given behavior. A major problem for developmentalists, however, is clearly detected in discussions of specific rather than general influences on development. That is, what changes (structure and/or process) occur as the organism ages? Answers from developmentalists are vague and too restrictive. The following contemporary developmental theories, although most popular, are subject to the criticisms of vagueness and restriction:

1. *Physiological maturation* (G. S. Hall, Gesell)—emphasis on maturational principles.
2. *Stage progression* (Bruner, Piaget, Werner)—emphasis on hypothetical constructs in attempting to explain adaptiveness of organism to a complex environment.
3. *Accumulation of higher-order capabilities* (Bijou, Fowler, Gagne, Jensen)—emphasis on learning principles (response-stimulus relationships).

The argument against employing the interaction postulate in attempting to explain phenotypes and phenotypic development is crucial. Although the interaction approach is appealing (e.g., "you can't have one without the other"), it does not aid much in delineating specific influences on development. The "in thing" is to reject either heredity or environment as a dominant influence on development and escape the question by stressing the all-encompassing interaction approach. Accepting the complex interaction of genes and physical and social environment theory does not, however, free the practitioner or researcher from *specifying* genetic and environmental influences.

SUMMARY LABELS EMPLOYED BY DEVELOPMENTALISTS

Bijou (1968), although erroneously excluding his own operant-respondent learning model, cautions the developmentalist's use of large, loosely defined constructs. Referring specifically to theorists employing stages of development, Bijou argues against labeling stages with hypothetical constructs. All too often, he claims, stage theorists attempt to explain behavior in terms of hypothetical constructs and environmental events. Riegel (1968) discussing the methodology of developmentalists and historians, has also subjected the concept of developmental stages to critical review. This criticism is important and may be applied to all attempts at model building. Not infrequently, students of behavior attempt to "explain" a given organismic action in terms of a hypothetical construct (an abstraction) which is based on the given action. This policy leads only to confusion. One cannot explain "something" by employing a construct that has not been defined or is part of the "something" to be explained. Perhaps the best example of such a practice is the classic one of the psychology student attempting to explain the irrational behavior of a person labeled psychotic. When asked *why* the person is performing in an irrational way, the student explains that it is because the individual is psychotic. The student confuses the issue of explanation versus description. Psychosis is a descriptive label (and nothing more!); it does not explain the descriptions. Piaget, for example, perhaps the most well-known contemporary theorist in developmental psychology, has been subjected to much criticism concerning the use of hypothetical "mental" constructs. Bijou and Riegel's criticisms of stage may be disregarded if this term is viewed as a *generic dependent variable*. That is, associated characteristics are incorporated as referents of a given stage or age.[3] The following doggerel by Van Den Daele (1969) indicates the relationship of various terms that may be classified as generic dependent variables:

> Milestones, phases, and ages
> render general gauges
> While periods, levels, and stages
> require pages and pages . . .
> (p. 303)

Milestones, phases, ages, periods, levels, and stages are generic dependent variables in that such terms are summary labels for specific behavioral referents that are highly correlated. That is, certain behaviors are characteristic of infants, other behaviors are characteristic of young children, other behaviors are characteristic of older children, and so on throughout the life span. The important point to remember is that specific behavioral referents define a given stage or period of development. Thus, generic dependent variables are only summary labels of more specific referents of developmental progression and regression. Again, remember that such generic dependent variables are for *descriptive* purposes; such variables do not *explain* anything.

Van Den Daele, employing the logic of set theory, suggests that summary

---

3. Baumeister (1967), citing problems in normal vs. mental retardation comparative studies, has also criticized age as an independent variable. Stating that mental age (MA) is not an entity but a product, Baumeister (p. 874) notes that "it is not uncommon to find such terms as 'attributed,' 'due to,' 'accounted for,' and even 'explained' used in connection with MA." As with chronological age, MA does not cause or explain anything—". . . to use MA as an explanatory construct would be circular" (Baumeister, 1967, p. 874).

labels which designate developmentally ordered characteristics correlate with the initial step of *developmental construct explication* or delineation. That is, an appropriate strategy for general and comprehensive representation of behavioral change includes the following steps:

1. Identification of obvious characteristics that distinguish the subject(s) developmentally;
2. Identification of empirical consistencies associated with characteristics of interest (revision of step 1 if new relationships emerge); and
3. Translation of steps 1 and 2 into a more general representational system (e.g., logical algebraic representation).

Van Den Daele notes that following the above strategy leads to "more comprehensive, yet precise descriptive-theoretical statements" (p. 304). Piaget's theory of cognitive adaptation is a good example of the above process of developmental construct explication. Piaget's (1970) theory consists of three principal periods of development:

1. *Sensorimotor period* (approximately birth to 1½ years of age);
2. *Concrete operations period* (approximately 2 to 11 years of age); and
3. *Propositional or formal operations period* (approximately 11 years of age through adolescence).

These three principle periods are further delineated:

1. *Sensorimotor period:* (a) subperiod of infant's centration on its own body; (b) subperiod of objectivization and spatialization of the schemes of practical intelligence.
2. *Concrete operations period:* (a) preoperational subperiod; (b) subperiod dealing with the beginnings of operational groupings in their various concrete forms and with their various types of conservation.
3. *Formal operations period:* (a) subperiod of organization; (b) subperiod of achievement of combinatory and group INRC (identity, negation, reciprocity, and correlativity) operations.

Finally, specific referents are provided within each subperiod of Piaget's developmental model. For the present purposes, delineation of the referents within the sensorimotor period should be sufficient:

1. *Sensorimotor period:*
    (a) subperiod of infant's centration on its own body:
    REFERENTS: (1) sensorimotor schemata—reflexive actions (orienting responses to stimuli); (2) primary circular reactions—simple habits (sucking response to non-feeding situations); and (3) sec-

ondary circular reactions—development of intentional schemes (representation of environmental events).

(b) subperiod of objectivization and spatialization of the schemes of practical intelligence:

REFERENTS: (1) coordination of secondary schemes—application of schemata to new situations; (2) tertiary circular reaction—manipulation of environment through experiment, interest in novel situations; and (3) representative intelligence—invention of new means to deal with the environment, transition to symbolic thought.

It is presently suggested that developmental designs (pre-experimental and experimental) provide a valuable methodological model for Van Den Daele's behavioral change strategy. That is, normative (descriptive) data supplies the developmentalist with specific interdependent characteristics or referents. Also, descriptive behavioral change research is important to the classic experimentalist. That is, such research emphasizes organismic change and aids in unconfounding "extraneous" (e.g., sex, socioeconomic class, age) effects from experimental treatment effects.

A final point in this *basic elements* section concerns the specific discipline of developmental psychology. In the past, developmental psychology has been most frequently equated with child development. Inhelder (1957) and Werner (1957), early critics of this isomorphism, proposed that the development construct may be applicable to all of behavior. Others have recently emphasized Inhelder and Werner's claim that students of developmental psychology may study change during any segment of the organism's living existence. *Aging research* and the *life-span model* argue against equating child and developmental problems on the basis that the type or age of the organism is not what determines whether a study is developmental. Kessen's (1960, p. 36) general formulation that "a characteristic is said to be developmental if it can be related to age in an orderly or lawful way" enables any segment of the life span to be open to developmental research.

Much of developmental investigation (i.e., research consisting of observing different age level samples in an attempt to obtain age-functional relationships) has centered on early periods in the life span marked by striking change—infancy, childhood, and adolescence. Students interested in this restricted period are referred to Mussen (1970) and Reese and Lipsitt's (1970) manuals on child psychology.

Although developmental psychologists have finally attempted to sever both the umbilical cord and apron string, the early fixation on child development has left many with restricted postulate systems and methods of inquiry. Although research and theoretical interest has expanded recently to include study of individuals at the final period of the life span (senescence), the many years between the beginning and end of life have not received much attention from developmentalists. In relation to this lack of research in adulthood, the young adult's criticism that no one understands him is rather accurate. Disciplines of human behavior have not stressed this period of the life span. In fact, behavioral researchers employ young adults (i.e., college students) as a means to an end. Such research is static in that emphasis is placed on general psychological laws and applications (e.g., learning, memory, perception). There is little concern with establishing basic knowledge on the young adult; rather, static behavioral research fails on two counts: (a) understanding the young adult as he interacts with his environment, and (b) subjecting behavioral models to developmental analyses.

The above discussion was an attempt to acquaint the student with the effort that is being made by numerous authors to integrate the various states of life—infancy, childhood, adolescence (development); adulthood (stability); old age (decline)—into a developmental psychology which covers the ontogenetic continuum. Quetelet (1835) was an initial contributor to this life span concept. In the early 1800s he hinted that progressive sequences of change are not restricted to a single period of life with the following statement: "man is born, grows up, and dies, according to certain laws which have never been properly investigated, either as a whole or in the mode of their mutual reactions" (1835, p. 1). Quetelet's candid remarks also point out an issue in the study of behavioral change with which this Primer is primarily concerned; i.e., developmental problems require proper investigative techniques. In the past, most developmental psychologists were content (and confident!) in borrowing research designs from other fields of scientific inquiry. Although it is readily admitted that developmental psychology is a loosely integrated discipline relying on concepts from genetics, physiology, endocrinology, pediatrics, psychiatry, anthropology, sociology, and psychology in general, students of developmental change have only recently expressed a demand for a developmental-specific research methodology.

CLASSICAL DEVELOPMENTAL DESIGNS

WITHIN THE LAST SEVERAL years there has been a rapid growth of creative output in research methodology pertaining to the analysis of developmental change. Many developmental psychologists have recognized inherent inadequacies found in the conventional *cross-sectional* (comparative measurement) and *longitudinal* (repeated measurement) designs. For a brief history and a detailed review of the advantages and disadvantages attributed to these classic models, students are referred to Baltes (1968) and Wohlwill (1969, 1970). The *cross-sectional* and *longitudinal* designs include identical parameters or dimensions and may be schematically depicted as follows:[4]

Longitudinal approach

$$\begin{bmatrix} S_1 & A_1 & O_1 & T_1 \\ S_1 & A_2 & O_2 & T_2 \\ S_1 & A_3 & O_3 & T_3 \\ \circ & \cdot & \cdot & \cdot \\ S_i & A_j & O_k & T_l \end{bmatrix} = S_i A_j O_k T_l$$

$i = 1$
$j = 1,2,3,\ldots, m$
$k = 1,2,3,\ldots, r$
$l = 1,2,3,\ldots, s$

Cross-sectional approach

$$\begin{bmatrix} S_1 & A_1 & O_1 & T_1 \\ S_2 & A_2 & O_1 & T_1 \\ S_3 & A_3 & O_1 & T_1 \\ \cdot & \cdot & \cdot & \cdot \\ S_i & A_j & O_k & T_l \end{bmatrix} = S_i A_j O_k T_l$$

$i = 1,2,3,\ldots, n$
$j = 1,2,3,\ldots, m$
$k = 1$
$l = 1$

where:

S_i = sample
A_j = age, level, grade
O_k = observation of dependent variable
T_l = time of measurement

CROSS-SECTIONAL DESIGN

Employing the *cross-sectional* design as an investigatory guide, samples (S_i) of different ages (A_j) are observed on a particular dependent variable once (O_k) at the same time of measurement (T_l). Normative data (e.g., motor, perceptual, speech development) stem from this basic design. Employing the simple *cross-sectional* design, the researcher measures a certain characteristic, say vocabulary size, over numerous age groups (e.g., 5-, 10-, 15-, and 20-year-olds). Assessment of vocabulary size across groups is conducted within a short period of time. Thus, all subjects (from all groups) are tested for vocabulary size at approximately the same time. It is also important to note that when the researcher is utilizing the *cross-sectional* design, he ends up with group *averages*;

---

4. Based on Baltes (1968) and Campbell and Stanley (1963).

i.e., average or mean vocabulary size of 5-year-olds, 10-year-olds, 15-year-olds, and 20-year-olds. For each group, each subject or individual score contributes to the average, or, more appropriately, each subject score goes into making up an average score for the group. If the researcher tests ten 5-year-olds, he may obtain the following range of vocabulary size scores:

Subject	Score
1	50
2	60
3	45
4	65
5	85
6	50
7	65
8	90
9	45
10	80

The mean or average for 5-year-olds is 63.50. As can be seen from the above distribution of scores, no subject has a score that is equal to the average. The mean only represents the *group's* average. Obviously, subjects within the group vary in terms of vocabulary-size scores. A simple example of a *cross-sectional* design is the following:

> A researcher wishes to ascertain the height of males and females throughout their postnatal life. Since age is a generic dependent variable, the researcher will test males and females at yearly intervals. Assuming the normal life span to be seventy years, the researcher will have to gather 140 samples (1 through 70 years for *both* males and females). If the researcher tests ten individuals within each sample (random selection), he will have to measure the height of 1,400 individuals. The above developmental problem can be depicted as follows:

Sample	Age	Sex	Dependent variable (height)
1	1 yr.	male	77 cm.
2	1	female	76
3	2	male	85
4	2	female	84
.	.	.	.
139	70	male	178
140	70	female	168

The important point to remember concerning the cross-sectional method is that the researcher (and his associates) must measure the height of individuals in *all* the samples at approximately the same time period (e.g., all subjects are measured within one month). The cross-sectional design is frequently employed in normative measures of weight, speech, and motor development.

The age variable does not identify a *cross-sectional* study. The *cross-sectional* design is basically a comparative one; i.e., comparison of two or more groups on a dependent variable. Each group in a comparative study is selected according to some *criterion*. The criterion may be age, as in the above *cross-sectional* study example, or any other characteristic that can be subjected to categorization— e.g., sex, race, socioeconomic status, IQ scores, etiology of mental retardation. The following example of a comparative or *cross-sectional* study is based on research in mental retardation. As you will note, several groups were employed in the study (Friedrich, Fuller, and Hawkins, 1969), selected on the basis of intelligence (mental age), chronological age, and etiology of mental retardation.

RELATIONSHIP BETWEEN PERCEPTION (INPUT) AND EXECUTION (OUTPUT)

Summary.—Fifteen brain-damaged and nine non-brain-damaged retarded subjects were given the following visual-motor tasks: (a) the Wechsler Intelligence Scale for Children Block Design subtest, (b) the Wechsler Intelligence Scale for Children Block Design multiple-choice procedure presented by Birch and his associates, and (c) the Minnesota Percepto-Diagnostic Test circle-diamond figures, incorporating pencil and block procedures. A combination of the Block Design subtest and the circle-diamond figures was successful in indicating subjects with execution (motor) or integrative dysfunctions. The multiple-choice procedure proved invalid as a technique for differentiating subjects with executive or integrative dysfunctions from subjects with visual perceptual difficulties. The results argue against the commonly held notion that perception is a unitary process. Rather, the findings suggest that failures on visual-motor tasks by mentally retarded subjects result primarily from faulty executive or integrative components (Friedrich, Fuller, and Hawkins, 1969, p. 923).

The subjects resided in an institution for the mentally retarded, and were placed in one of two groups (brain-damaged, non-brain-damaged) based on the American Association of Mental Deficiency's (Heber, 1959, 1971) classification system. That is, the subject's diagnosis (type of mental retardation) was based on neurological examinations conducted by practicing neurologists and other available medical history. The two groups were established on the basis of neurological criteria. Two other variables employed in the study—chronological age and IQ—were not used to differentiate subjects. No significant difference was found between groups on chronological age. This simply means that the brain-damaged (mean age 17.77 years) and non-brain-damaged (mean age 16.82 years) groups consisted of subjects that were of approximately the same age. With the IQ variable, however, a significant difference was found between groups which favored the non-brain-damaged group (mean IQ for brain-damaged subjects 50.93; mean IQ for non-brain-damaged subjects 67.67). This finding means that IQ or intelligence is a confounding variable; any significant difference in *task performance* between brain-damaged and non-brain-damaged groups cannot be accounted for on the basis of etiology alone. Since non-brain-damaged subjects are significantly more intelligent than brain-damaged subjects in the present study, the general intellectual factor may account for part or all of the significant difference between groups on a particular performance. In the Friedrich, Fuller, and Hawkins study no significant difference was found between groups on performance on the *multiple-choice Block Design* procedure. A significant difference between groups was found on performance on the *Minnesota Percepto-Diagnostic* test. Although non-brain-damaged subjects performed significantly better than brain-damaged subjects, the former had a significantly higher mean IQ. Thus, the significant mean group performance difference is confounded by the significant mean group IQ difference. A researcher can avoid this confounding problem by employing a factorial design with the following groups:

	IQ	
	low	high
brain-damaged	1	2
non-brain-damaged	3	4

For any given task, the following comparisons may be made: (a) 1-2, (b) 1-3, (c) 1-4, (d) 2-3, (e) 2-4, (f) 3-4. Two other procedures may be employed to avoid IQ variable confounding: (a) match subjects from both groups on IQ; and (b) restrict the IQ range for both groups. The researcher can also deal with the possible IQ confounding effect statistically (which was done in the Friedrich, Fuller, and Hawkins study)—e.g., employing an analysis of covariance to partial out the confounding variable effect.

LONGITUDINAL DESIGN

Within the *longitudinal* design, one sample (S_i) is observed on two or more occasions (O_k^r) on a particular dependent variable at different ages (A_j^m) and thus at different times of measurement (T_l^s). Utilizing *age* as a generic dependent variable, the following is a hypothetical example of a *longitudinal* design:

> A research program may be initiated to ascertain the height of males and females throughout their postnatal life. As you will note, this developmental issue was discussed in a previous hypothetical example depicting the *cross-sectional* design. Employing the *longitudinal* design, however, the researcher selects a sample of males and females (e.g., ten in each group) before the first year after birth. Within this longitudinal program, the *same* subjects (ten males, ten females) are measured yearly (age 1 through 70). Thus, employing this repeated measures design, only twenty subjects are studied throughout their lifetime. A *longitudinal* framework can be depicted as follows:

Sample	Age	Sex	Dependent variable (height)
1	1 yr.	male	77 cm.
	2	male	85
	.	.	.
	70	male	178
2	1	female	76
	2	female	84
	.	.	.
	70	female	168

Utilizing the *longitudinal* design to record height for males and females 1 through 70, the researchers would have to record height measures for 70 years. It is probably obvious from the height examples that the *longitudinal* design may be an impractical one (e.g., time, cost, staff turnover, subject loss). This is not, however, always the case. Usually, many dependent variables are included within a major *longitudinal* program. That is, such programs include repeated measures of individual (e.g., IQ, attitudes, values, personality) attributes. Two major American *longitudinal* programs often are referenced in developmental research and theory: University of California (including Berkeley Growth Study, Berkeley Guidance Study, and Oakland Growth Study) and Stanford University (Terman's studies of the gifted). A general conclusion regarding the two classical developmental designs is the following: *Cross-sectional* designs incorporate few (often only one) dependent variables, whereas *longitudinal* designs incorporate many dependent variables. Kagan (1964) has summarized the samples, methods, and goals of ten major American *longitudinal* projects that have been active for many years. Kagan's summarization of one of these programs, Terman's Study of the Gifted Child, should prove helpful to students interested in the basic mechanics of *longitudinal* programs.

CONDENSED SUMMARY OF PROJECT

Composition and social origin of group. The subjects in this famous study were enrolled at an average age of 11 years, although the total range was 3 to 18 years of age. The original contact was made during 1921-1922, and follow-up studies occurred in 1927-1928, 1939-1940, 1950-1952, with questionnaire contact in 1924, 1925, 1936, 1940, 1945, 1955, and 1960. Aside from the intelligence test data, the major sources of additional information came from interviews and questionnaires supplied by the subjects, parents, and teachers. A detailed description of this project is available in four of the five volumes entitled "The Genetic Studies of Genius" published by the Stanford University Press.

The subjects were selected from the State of California after a systematic search for gifted children. The total group included 857 males and 671 females. Approximately 80 per cent of the parents were born in the United States; the 20 per cent foreign-born represented twenty-five countries. Ten per cent of the subjects were of Jewish background, .8 per cent Oriental (either one or both parents), and .2 per cent Negro. Data on the religious composition of the families are incomplete.

About 45 per cent of the fathers and 30 per cent of the mothers had some college training; one-third of the fathers and 15 per cent of the mothers graduated from college, while 43 per cent of the fathers and 42 per cent of the mothers did not graduate from high school. The distribution of paternal vocations in 1922 included 31 per cent professional, 27 per cent semiprofessional and higher business, 24 per cent clerical, skilled trades, and retail business, 7 per cent farming, and 11 per cent semiskilled and minor clerical occupations.

CHILDHOOD AND ADULT INFORMATION

Mental tests. For selection purposes (1921-1922) the Stanford-Binet was given to 1,070 subjects, the Terman Group Test of Mental Ability to 428 subjects, the National Intelligence Test to 24 subjects, and the Army Alpha to 6 subjects. Tests of school achievement were given to 955 subjects.

Retests of intelligence were administered in 1927-1928, using the Stanford-Binet for children under 13 years of age and the Terman Group Test for the older subjects. In 1939-1940 and 1950-1952, the Concept Mastery Test was given to approximately 1000 subjects and 700 spouses.

Personality inventories. A battery of character and personality and interest tests was administered to subjects in 1921-1922 and 1927-1928.

The material quoted above and elsewhere in this book from J. Kagan, "American longitudinal research in psychological development," *Child Development*, 1964, 35, pp. 25-27, used by permission of the Society for Research in Child Development, Inc.

In 1939-1940 the Personality and Temperament Test and Test of Marital Happiness were given to 652 subjects and spouses. The Personality and Temperament Test was also given to 375 unmarried subjects. The Marital Happiness Test was given in 1950-1952 to 908 subjects and 540 Spouses.

The Strong Vocational Interest Test was taken by 627 men and 200 women of the Terman group in 1939-1940.

Further information on personality at various stages is available from trait ratings of the subjects by parents and teachers in 1921-1922 and 1927-1928, by parents and spouses in 1939-1940, and from self-ratings on traits in 1939-1940 and 1950-1952. Field workers supplied trait ratings in 1939-1940 and 1950-1952. An eight-page biographical data blank was filled out by 1,119 subjects in 1950-1952.

Interviews. The child was interviewed initially when the project started (i.e., 1921-1922) and on three later occasions (1927-1928, 1939-1940, and 1950-1952).

One or both parents were interviewed in 1922, 1928, and 1940. The teachers were interviewed in 1922 and 1928. Ratings and summaries are available from these interviews. These dealt with such variables as parental punishment and reward, parental goals for child, and the child's behavior, interests, and attitudes towards peers. At all stages the inquiry has been directed toward obtaining a continuing record on health, nervous tendencies, personal and social adjustments, nature of interests and activities, as well as educational, vocational, and marital histories.

THE SECOND GENERATION

Stanford-Binet tests have been given to approximately 1,600 offspring of the gifted subjects. For about 75 per cent of these, an information blank calling for the early developmental and childhood data was filled out by the mother (p. 25-27).

Four important identifying characteristics of longitudinal programs that are illustrated nicely in Kagan's summary of Terman's program are the following:

1. Repeated measurement: 1921-1922, 1924, 1925, 1927-1928, 1936, 1939-1940, 1940, 1945, 1950-1952, 1955, and 1960.
2. Multiple dependent measures: IQ, personality, school achievement, and interest tests.
3. Numerous subject data sources: gifted subjects, parents, and teachers.
4. University affiliation: Stanford University, Department of Psychology.

PROBLEMS OF CLASSICAL DESIGNS

A critical difference between the two classical designs is the use of independent sampling ($\overset{n}{S_i}$) in the *cross-sectional* method and dependent sampling (S_i) in the *longitudinal* method (Baltes, 1968). This difference reflects the repeated measurement principle operating within *longitudinal* programs; subject characteristics measured at time 2 are compared with characteristics measured previously (time 1). Dependent sampling results in confounded effects—biased data—which will be discussed in detail in a later section. Kessen (1960) provides the following example of hypothetical data which depicts the difference between dependent and independent sampling:

> ... an examination of the fictitious data in Table 2 will illustrate [the difference in sampling procedures] between the [cross-sectional and longitudinal] methods and one of its implications.

TABLE 2
FICTITIOUS DATA WHICH ILLUSTRATE THE "MATCHED GROUP" CHARACTERISTIC OF LONGITUDINAL RESEARCH DESIGN

	A			B	
	Scores at Age a	Scores at Age a + t		Scores at Age a	Scores at Age a + t
	4	5		4	13
	5	6		5	14
	6	7		6	15
	7	8		7	16
	8	9		8	17
	9	10		9	18
	10	11		10	19
	11	12		11	20
	12	13		12	21
Mean Score	8	9	Mean Score	8	17

> If there are small but reliable changes in the behaviors of subjects over age (Table 2A), then longitudinal study provides, because of the matching characteristic, more sensitive estimates of such changes. When the differences between groups are large (Table 2B), the advantage of the longitudinal technique is less impressive. Making the point more generally, we may say that the longitudinal design is to be favored in the study of those age-functional relationships in which relatively small but individually stable changes over age are expected [Kessen, 1960, pp. 41-42].

Both classical developmental research strategies—*cross-sectional, longitudinal*—can be represented by Kessen's (1960) unidimensional formula:

R = f (A)

where:

R = (response) dependent variable(s) (physical or psychological), defined by the measurement instrument(s) used;

A = (age) independent variable, representing different levels of organismic adaptation to the environment.

A PRIMER FOR DEVELOPMENTAL METHODOLOGY

Utilizing the unidimensional formula, R = f(A), significant differences found between age groups (e.g., 5- vs. 10-year-olds) are often interpreted as due to the age or maturational factor. As noted by Kessen (1960, p. 36), age "represents not only time since birth but includes as well such referents as physiological age and mental age."

Although developmental research relies almost exclusively on the classical designs, such methods of data collection are classified as pre-experimental designs (Campbell and Stanley, 1963). As Baltes (1968) has noted, pre-experimental designs have important methodological deficiencies. More specifically, such designs incorporate factors jeopardizing internal and external validity. For clarification, internal validity deals with independent variable manipulation and external validity deals with the generalizability of independent-dependent relationships. As will become clear below, internal and external validity may be somewhat incompatible criteria in a given study. In a simple sense, internal validity refers to the utility of a given independent manipulation. The question raised here is: Did the independent variable contribute solely to variation in the dependent variable? At issue is experimental control. If a researcher is interested in a given independent-dependent relationship, he must control for possible extraneous effects, i.e., control for other variables that may affect a given dependent variable. If a researcher does not exercise control, he may end up with confounded results; dependent variable changes that may be due to factors other than independent variable manipulation. An example of such confounding in developmental research is the following.

> A researcher tested for possible differences between 5- and 10-year-olds in egocentric behavior. Two samples were drawn, twenty subjects in each age group. The researcher obtained his 5-year-olds from a day care center for families on welfare. The 10-year-olds were obtained from a university affiliated elementary laboratory school. An analysis of the data indicated that 5-year-olds were significantly more egocentric than 10-year-olds. Obviously, the age variable is often employed as a criterion in developmental research. A serious question raised in terms of internal validity concerns possible socioeconomic variable confounding. University-affiliated elementary schools cater to children of university professors. Since the researcher did not control for socioeconomic status in the egocentrism study, he does not know whether or not this variable accounted for some or all of the difference in scores between age groups. The point raised: Did age and/or socioeconomic status account for the significant difference?

In the case of external validity, the researcher is concerned with the extent to which he can generalize his findings. Studies, based on samples, are conducted with the goal of generalizing findings to target populations. As noted by Bracht and Glass (1968, pp. 437-438): "To the extent and manner in which the results of an experiment can be generalized to different subjects, settings, experimenters, and possibly, tests, the experiment possesses *external validity*." Factors jeopardizing external validity, summarized by Bracht and Glass (pp. 438-439), are the following:

I. Population Validity
  A. Experimentally Accessible Population vs. Target Population: Generalizing from the population of subjects that is available to the experimenter (the accessible population) to the total population of subjects about whom he is interested (the target population) requires a thorough knowledge of the characteristics of both populations. The results of an experiment might apply only for those special sorts of persons from whom the experimental subjects were selected and not for some larger population of persons.
  B. Interaction of Personological Variables and Treatment Effects: If the superiority of one experimental treatment over another would be reversed when subjects at a different level of some variable descriptive of persons are exposed to the treatments, there exists an interaction of treatment effects and personological variable.

II. Ecological Validity
  A. Describing the Independent Variable Explicitly: Generalization and replication of the experimental results presuppose a complete knowledge of all aspects of the treatment and experimental setting.
  B. Multipe-Treatment Interference:: When two or more treatments are administered consecutively to the same persons within the same or different studies, it is difficult and sometimes impossible to ascertain the cause of the experimental results or to generalize the results to settings in which only one treatment is present.
  C. Hawthorne Effect: A subject's behavior may be influenced partly by his perception of the experiment and how he should respond to the experimental stimuli. His awareness of participating in an experiment may precipitate behavior which would not occur in a setting which is not perceived as experimental.
  D. Novelty and Disruption Effects: The experimental results may be due partly to the enthusiasm or disruption generated by the newness of the treatment. The effect of some new program in a setting where change is common may be quite different from the effect in a setting where few changes have been experienced.
  E. Experimenter Effect: The behavior of the subjects may be unintentionally influenced by certain characteristics or behaviors of the experimenter. The expectations of the experimenter may also bias the administration of the treatment and the observation of the subjects' behavior.
  F. Pretest Sensitization: When a pretest has been administered, the experimental results may partly be a result of the sensitization to the content of the treatment. The results of the experiment might not apply to a second group of persons who were not pretested.

G. *Post-test Sensitization:* Treatment effects may be latent or incomplete and appear only when a post-experimental test is administered.
H. *Interaction of History and Treatment Effects:* The results may be unique because of "extraneous" events occurring at the time of the experiment.
I. *Measurement of the Dependent Variable:* Generalization of the results depends on the identification of the dependent variables and the selection of instruments to measure these variables.
J. *Interaction of Time of Measurement and Treatment Effects:* Measurement of the dependent variable at two different times may produce different results. A treatment effect which is observed immediately after the administration of the treatment may not be observed at some later time, and vice versa.

Although the classical developmental designs are classified as pre-experimental, such designs have proved to be valuable tools for developmentalists. The *cross-sectional* design is regarded as appropriate for (a) purposes of immediate prediction and control (Schaie, 1959), and (b) obtaining normative characteristics and trends of central tendency and variability (Bayley, 1956). The second advantage of *cross-sectional* designs—obtaining normative characteristics and trends of central tendency and variability—refers to *inter-individual* variation. Since the *cross-sectional* design is basically comparative in nature, it is employed for analyzing possible group mean differences. More specifically, dependent variable inter-individual variability consists of variation among subjects of a given group (within-group variability) and dependent variable variation across groups (between-group variability). Usually, the latter type of variability is of concern to the researcher dealing with age-related dependent variables. Between-group or experimental variance refers to systematic differences across age groups on dependent variables. The following criticism of the *cross-sectional* method, succinctly expressed by Baltes and Goulet (1970, pp. 16-17), should be given serious consideration by both students and professionals:

...A cross-sectional study...must be considered as a weak strategy as long as more information is desired than the comparison of mean differences between age samples. Moreover, conventional cross-sectional studies (particularly, when covering the life span) are bound to confound age differences with a number of uncontrolled factors, e.g., individual differences in life span (selective survival), differences between generations, or age-specific selective sampling effects which preclude the comparability of the age groups involved. Thus, only in rare instances can it be assumed that cross-sectional age differences are a result of the aging process, that is, do reflect age changes. What is necessary in research of this nature is the incorporation of a series of control groups to check the assumption that age differences obtained using cross-sectional designs reflect *average* and unbiased intra-individual age changes.

The *longitudinal* design is viewed as uniquely effective in the exploration of (a) individual identity, (b) temporal patterning of changes within a given individual on a given variable, and (c) patterning of the relationships among variables changing over time within a given individual (Baltes, 1968; Thomas, Chess, Birch, Hertsizk, and Korn, 1963). Wohlwill (1969) delineates the three types of information preserved by the *longitudinal* design as follows:

1. *Individual identity:* "merely indicates the fact that longitudinal data are dependent measures, i.e., that they allow us to place data at time t_1 into one-for-one correspondence with those at time t_2. This dependence has an effect, of course, on tests of significance for age differences and on the power of these tests in particular. However, retention of individual-identity information has a further important advantage in age-level comparisons besides decreasing the errors estimates in tests of significance: it ensures identity of the population at the various age levels, whereas cross-sectional comparisons not only typically involve cohort generation differences, but frequently differences in other respects, e.g., between the populations represented by a particular grade school and a particular high school in the same town, or between a sample of college students and a sample of older persons present at a single institution. These are, of course, matters subject to some control, but the practical difficulties in the way of obtaining comparable samples in different age groups over an extended age span are not to be minimized" (pp. 22-23).
2. *Temporal patterning of changes within a given individual on a given variable:* "concerns aspects of the temporal patterning of responses for a given individual—information which is apt to become obscured when group-average cross-sectional design data are relied on. Rate of change and, above all, shape of the developmental function are examples of such temporal-patterning data subject to distortion through group averaging" (p. 23).
3. *Patterning of the relationships among variables changing over time within a given individual:* "concerning intra-individual patterning of relationships among variables over time . . . there is . . . no substitute for the longitudinal method at all. Wherever we are concerned with relationships between amount or direction of change for two or more variables, or between such change and any other information about the individual, we are necessarily forced to resort to the longitudinal method" (p. 26).

Although this Primer deals with methodological deficiencies inherent in the classical developmental designs, students should be aware of the practical difficulties associated with longitudinal designs. Wohlwill (1969, p. 28), in the following quote, expresses quite nicely the practical problems facing longitudinal programs:

The material quoted above and elsewhere in this book from J. F. Wohlwill, 1969. Methodology and research strategy in the study of developmental change. *Educational Testing Service Research Memorandum*, used by permission of the author.

The practical obstacles to be overcome in undertaking. longitudinal work cannot be overestimated, to be sure. They range from such seemingly trivial problems as that of adequate data storage and record-keeping (which undoubtedly can be a source of many headaches, particularly for long-term studies involving a wide assortment of measures) to the ultimately much more critical difficulties of administering a research project over a span of a generation or more, in the face of turnover of personnel, change in interests on the part of those associated with the project, and, most serious, perhaps, changes in the status of knowledge, techniques, etc., taking place over the course of the project, which can rarely be assimilated into the study, once it has been launched. In brief: change may operate on the investigator at the same rate as on his subjects, and it operates on his tools and the state of the field at a very much faster rate. Problems of aging, in other words, beset a longitudinal study along with its subjects, causing it to diminish in value and usefulness, long before the latter's entire life span is covered.

Although both conventional strategies were expected to produce similar age difference and/or age change results, this expectation was infrequently borne out (Baltes and Nesselroade, 1969). The reader interested in contradictory *cross-sectional* and *longitudinal* findings is referred to Botwinick's (1970) review of geropsychology. In regard to contradictory findings, Schaie (1970, p. 489) reviewed various *longitudinal* and *cross-sectional* studies dealing with specific variables. His inferences are presented in Table 3.

Schaie's review clearly indicates the problem of classic developmental design bias. Inherent methodological deficiencies (resulting in divergent findings) and/or practical disadvantages of the conventional developmental designs have been frequently noted.[5] Recent methodological standards presented by Baltes (1968), Baltes and Nesselroade (1970), Goulet and Baltes (1970), Gottman, McFall, and Barnett (1969), Harris (1963), Schaie (1965, 1970), Solomon and Lessac (1968), and Wohlwill (1970a, 1970b) point out the naiveté of the classical behavioral change designs.

Discrepant findings (resulting from methodological deficiencies) and practical problems have accented the need for evaluating the basic assumptions of *longitudinal* and *cross-sectional* strategies. Baltes (1968), Kessen (1960), and Schaie (1965, 1970) have presented the most damaging criticism directed at classical approaches. These developmental psychologists have indicated that the emphasis on simple age functions, $R = f(A)$, found in the conventional unidimensional designs results in a disregard for delineating other sources of variance. Both designs thus produce an age main effect and confounded sources of error. The following analysis of variance model example may be of assistance

---

5. See starred items in the References at the end of this Primer for articles and books dealing with developmental design.

TABLE 3

COMPARISON OF INFERENCES DRAWN FROM CROSS-SECTIONAL, LONGITUDINAL, AND SHORT-TERM LONGITUDINAL STUDIES[a]

Variable	Cross-sectional	Longitudinal	Short-term longitudinal
Verbal meaning	Sharp decrement from middle adulthood to old age	Modest gain throughout life from young adult plateau	Modest decrement from young adult plateau; increment in successive cohorts reaching asymptote
Space	Sharp decrement from young adult peak to old age	Modest decrement from adult plateau	Almost no decrement until advanced age; steep positive cohort gradient is reaching asymptote
Reasoning	Sharp decrement from young adult peak to old age	Modest gain from young adult plateau till old age	Modest decrement from middle adulthood to old age; positively accelerating cohort gradient
Number	Modest gain and loss before and subsequent to mid-life plateau	Modest gain from early adulthood to plateau at advanced age	Very modest decrement from plateau in middle adulthood; positively accelerated cohort gradient
Word fluency	Moderate decrement from plateau extending over major portion of adulthood	Moderate gains from young adult levels	Sharp decrements from young adult levels; steep decrements for successive cohorts

[a] Inferences from cross-sectional data are based on data by Kamin (1957), H. E. Jones (1959), and Schaie (1958). No long-term longitudinal studies on the PMA variables were found, but inferences are based on an examination of analogous data available from studies by Bayley (1968b), Bayley and Oden (1955), and Owens (1953). The short-term longitudinal inferences are those of Schaie and Strother (1968a, 1968b).

to readers with little knowledge of variance components. A mathematical model is associated with a given design and purports to include all sources of variability (variance) affecting individual scores. If a given mathematical model accurately represents sources of variability, the effects of a treatment (independent variable) can be evaluated. The *completely randomized design* is the simplest experimental design employing the randomization principle. The linear model for completely randomized design is:

$X_{ij} = \mu + \beta_j + \xi_{ij}$. According to this model, an individual score (X_{ij}) = the population mean (μ) + a treatment effect (β_j) + an error effect (ξ_{ij}). It is important here to note that an error effect is unique for each subject and is an estimate of all effects not attributable to a particular treatment level. The researcher, by employing appropriate designs and experimental controls, attempts to minimize the size of the error effect (i.e., that portion of variance not attributable to a particular treatment level). If the researcher has one treatment (e.g., age), the appropriate model is $X_{ij} = \mu + \beta_j + \xi_{ij}$. If, however, there are two treatment effects (e.g., age and socioeconomic status), the appropriate design is $X_{ijk} = \mu + \alpha_i + \beta_j + \alpha\beta_{ij} + \xi_{ijk}$. It should be obvious that if the researcher employs the one factor design when, in fact, he has two factors operating, the error term will confound β_j, $\alpha\beta_{ij}$ and error. Thus, in this example, the researcher has not attributed variance to the appropriate effects.

Kessen (1960) proposed that the classical designs, emphasizing simple age-functional relationships, lack the following specifications that a meaningful design for developmental research must include:

1. age interacting with particular populations;
2. age interacting with environmental change; and
3. age interacting simultaneously with environmental and population differences.

The specification of age interacting with particular populations is depicted in the following paradigm: R = f (A, P), where A refers to age and P refers to population. Quite simply, the R = f (A, P) paradigm lets the researcher manipulate two variables: age (invariant) and a subgroup defined by a qualitative phenotype (variant). The subgroup variable most often manipulated in developmental research is sex. A schematic example of a research design within the R = f (A, P) paradigm is as follows:

		Sex		
		Male	Female	
Age Groups	7	S_1	S_2	
	10	S_3	S_4	S_i = sample
	14	S_5	S_6	
	17	S_7	S_8	

In the above diagram there are four age groups (7-,10-,14-,17-year-olds) and two sex groups. This 4 x 2 design requires eight samples. Age is usually referred to as a "between subjects" variable and sex (or any special population) is referred to as a "within subjects" variable. Other subgroup variables (P) that are often manipulated in developmental research include race, socioeconomic status, species, and culture. It is important to note that utilizing the R = f (A, P) paradigm enables the researcher to control for two variables. In the above diagram, sex is a controlled rather than confounding variable. If a researcher included males and females in a study and employed the R = f (A) unidimensional paradigm, sex may be a confounding variable. Obviously, utilizing the bidimensional R = f (A, P) paradigm does not exclude the possibility of a third confounding variable (e.g., socioeconomic status).

Kessen's second advanced paradigm, R = f (A, S) emphasizes age (A) interacting with environmental change (S). This interactional paradigm is based on two types of research settings: (a) *experimental manipulation,* and (b) *variation in conditions.* The former setting, a classic experimental approach, incorporates the advantage of random assignment of subjects to treatment (independent variable) conditions. As Kessen notes, most developmental studies utilizing *experimental manipulation* deal with *learning* variables. Since most learning studies have repeated measures of dependent variables (assess performance at time t_1, t_2, t_3, etc.), manipulation of the age variable permits such studies to be categorized as developmental. A hypothetical example of experimental manipulation within bidimensional R = f (A, S) is the following:

Study Conditions

	Experimental	Control	
Age Groups 7	S_1	S_2	
10	S_3	S_4	S_i = sample
14	S_5	S_6	
17	S_7	S_8	

In the above diagram, the experimental groups ($S_{1,3,5,7}$) are given the treatment (independent variable) and the control groups ($S_{2,4,6,8}$) do not receive the experimental treatment. The researcher, utilizing the above design, may analyze for possible differences among experimental groups ($S_{1,3,5,7}$), control groups ($S_{2,4,6,8}$), and within age groups (S_1-S_2, S_3-S_4, S_5-S_6, S_7-S_8). The randomization factor associated with *experimental manipulation* in developmental investigations is important enough to state again: subjects within ages are randomly assigned to study conditions (experimental, control). The second research setting with the R = f (A, S) paradigm, *variation in environmental conditions,* does not incorporate the randomization feature. In fact, the *variation in conditions setting* is isomorphic to the R = f (A, P) paradigm discussed earlier, with the stipulation that the *variation in conditions* method emphasizes antecedent natural environmental differences among subgroups. Institutionalization and child-rearing practice are variables that have been frequently employed in the *variation in conditions* research design.

The third advanced paradigm for developmental investigation proposed by Kessen, $R = f(A, P, S)$, is simply a combination of the $R = f(A, P)$ and $R = f(A, S)$ paradigms. Utilizing the *experimental manipulation* aspect of the $R = f(A, S)$ paradigm, the following diagram depicts a research design based on the $R = f(A, P, S)$ paradigm:

		Study Condition			
		Control		Experimental	
		Sex		Sex	
		Male	Female	Male	Female
Age Groups	7	S_1	S_2	S_3	S_4
	10	S_5	S_6	S_7	S_8
	14	S_9	S_{10}	S_{11}	S_{12}
	17	S_{13}	S_{14}	S_{15}	S_{16}

S_i = sample

With the above 4 (age) x 2 (sex) x 2 (conditions) design, the researcher may make numerous group comparisons: age variable, condition and sex constant (e.g., S_3, S_7, S_{11}, S_{15}; S_2, S_6, S_{10}, S_{14}); sex variable, age and condition constant (e.g., S_1, S_2; S_{15}, S_{16}); condition variable, age and sex constant (e.g., S_1, S_3; S_{14}, S_{16}).

With an introduction to the classical developmental designs, it is mandatory to discuss the methodological inadequacies inherent in *cross-sectional* and *longitudinal* methods. Baltes (1968, pp. 149-153) has provided an excellent discussion of the following specific methodological shortcomings associated with confounded sources of error in unifactorial developmental designs:

Selective sampling. Because of the repeated participation which is required of subjects in a longitudinal study, longitudinal samples almost always fail to meet criteria of representative sampling. Conversely, cross-sectional samples usually can fulfill this requirement without difficulty. Some empirical studies (Baker, Sontag, and Nelson, 1958; Kodlin and Thompson, 1958; Rose, 1965; Streib, 1966) demonstrate that longitudinal samples already from their onset run the risk of being selectively biased in a positive direction. For example, subjects who volunteer for longitudinal studies tend to be of a higher average intelligence and tend to be of a higher socioeconomic status. Such selective sampling biases in longitudinal studies impair (a) the comparability of cross-sectional and longitudinal investigations, and (b) the generalizability of longitudinal findings.

Selective survival. The phenomenon of selective survival applies to longitudinal as well as to cross-sectional samples. Selective survival implies that a given population at birth (cohort) changes in its composition in

---

The material quoted above and elsewhere in this book from P. B. Baltes. 1968. Longitudinal and cross-sectional sequences in the study of age and generation effects. *Human Development*, Vol. 11, used by permission of the publisher.

conjunction with the aging process as a result of death or incapacitation (Birren, 1959; Campbell and Stanley, 1963; Damon, 1965; Jarvik and Falek, 1963; Riegel, Riegel, and Meyer, 1967a, 1967b). This population change is selective to the extent that the survival rate is correlated with the measurement variables. Birren (1959, p. 30) pointed out that "survivors might be, for example, taller or shorter, brighter or duller, happier or unhappier than their non-surviving cohort." This assumption of selective survival is further substantiated by the well-known fact that members of certain psychopathological groups have a shorter life expectancy. Subsequently, Damon (1965) has demonstrated that alone on the basis of a negative correlation between height and life expectancy, the average height of older subjects tends to be less than that of younger subjects. Riegel, Riegel, and Meyer (1967b) describe a gerontological study in which the survivors were on the average more intelligent, less dogmatic and less rigid than the non-survivors. In such cases of selective survival, the age samples no longer represent the population of birth cohorts and are therefore biased. As was suggested in the case of selective sampling, the effect of selective survival tends to be in the direction of positive selection.

Selective drop-out. Whereas theoretically the different age groups of a longitudinal study are completely homogeneous, in reality they become heterogeneous due to drop-outs. Such drop-outs, in the sense of Campbell and Stanley's (1963) concept *experimental mortality*, occur during the course of the experiment as some subjects lose interest, change their residence, etc. This drop-out can be called selective if the loss of subjects does not follow a random pattern, i.e., if there is a correlation between the dependent variable and the characteristics related to drop-out. Selective drop-out, as defined here, is a characteristic of the sample under investigation and not a characteristic of the underlying population from which it was drawn. This is in contrast to the case of selective survival where attrition can be attributed to changes in both the underlying population and the sample.

As a consequence of selective drop-out, the longitudinal sample as measured later in the experiment $[S_1A_jO_kT_1]$ is no longer comparable to the original sample $[S_1A_1O_1T_1]$. Again in the case of selective drop-out, it has been shown that the sample seems to become progressively more and more biased in a positive direction (Ames and Walker, 1965; Anderson and Cohen, 1939).

Testing effects. The problem area of testing effects again applies primarily to the longitudinal method. The longitudinal designs, plans with repeated measurement, have as a basic assumption that the repeated observation of the same sample $[S_1O_1 - S_1O_k]$ has no effects on the dependent variable. This assumption is highly improbable for many psychological variables when one considers short- and long-term practice and satiation effects. Such effects have been demonstrated with achievement tests (e.g., Anastasi, 1958) as well as with personality tests (e.g., Windle, 1954). In connection with the longitudinal design, practice effects combined with increased test-sophistication and deliberate coaching have been cited as sources of error (Anastasi, 1958; Anderson, 1954; Kodlin and Thompson, 1958; Kuhlen, 1963; Miles, 1934; Owens, 1953; Sontag, Baker, and Nelson, 1958; Welford, 1961, 1964). The importance of testing effects as confounding variables should not be underestimated since many longitudinal studies employ a high number of retests. For example, in the well-known Berkeley Growth Study the majority of subjects were tested no less than 38 times over a period of 18 years (Bayley, 1949).

As a matter of fact, it is relatively easy to control testing effects in longitudinal studies by introducing adequate control groups. For the purpose of controlling testing effects, it is necessary only to draw two or more equivalent samples at the beginning of a longitudinal study and to vary them systematically in terms of number of observations made in the sense of a "posttest-only control group design" (Baltes, 1967; Campbell and Stanley, 1963; Schaie, 1965). In a later section dealing with the simultaneous application of longitudinal and cross-sectional sequences we will refer more explicitly to such a research plan.

Generation effects. The issue of generation effects as a source of error impairs the internal validity of cross-sectional studies and the external validity of longitudinal designs. With respect to the cross-sectional method it has been argued (Birren, 1959; Damon, 1965; Jerome, 1959; Kuhlen, 1963; Rosler, 1966; Schaie, 1965; Welford, 1964) that the age samples S_1A_1 - S_nA_m differ not only with regard to age, but also simultaneously as to generations in the sense of cohorts. First formulated by Kuhlen (1940), this issue has been stated more precisely by Anastasi (1958, p. 220): "Differences between 20- and 40-year-olds tested simultaneously (in 1940 or 1960) would reflect age changes plus cultural differentials, especially differences in the conditions under which the two age groups were reared." The relationship between age and generation effects in the cross-sectional design is presented in Figure 1.

In Figure 1 the broken lines represent the hypothetical average developmental gradients for the generations 1900-1950 for the age range from 10-60 years. These developmental gradients are based on two assumptions concerning the dependent variable: (a) age development as a linear progression, and (b) an acceleration from generation to generation. In a cross-sectional study conducted in 1960 there is available only one observation per cohort at a specific age level. The cohort of 1900 is observed at the age of 60, the cohort of 1910 at the age of 50, the cohort of 1920 at the age of 40, etc. The resulting age curve (solid line) corresponds neither to any of the single developmental gradients nor to the average of all of them. Therefore, if generation effects are present, the results of a cross-sectional study cannot be interpreted as pure age effects. In the obtained sample differences $[S_1A_1O_1T_1 - S_nA_mO_1T_1]$, age effects and generation effects are confounded. This confounding might take various forms. The example in Figure 1 was chosen since it explains the well-known textbook age curves of intelligence as a function of the interaction between age and generation effects, whereas usually this curve is interpreted as a function of age alone.

The sample differences of a longitudinal study $[S_1A_1O_1T_1 - S_1A_jO_kT_1]$ have been obtained from a single generation. Consequently, the age effect of a longitudinal study is generation specific. Therefore, the internal validity of a longitudinal design is not attenuated by the existence of generation differences. The external validity of age effects, however, found in longitudinal studies is seriously restricted. If, for example, the results of the Berkeley Growth Study, begun in 1928, are to be generalized to the birth cohort 1965, the generation gap is almost forty years.

In summary, one must conclude that the conventional methods are in no way adequate research designs for the assessment of age effects. Due to the various methodological deficiencies it is not legitimate to interpret the sample differences obtained in longitudinal and cross-sectional studies as pure age effects. Besides the age effects a number of other uncontrolled sources of variance are confounded. These uncontrolled factors are alternative explanations for the obtained sample differences. The picture can become very complicated indeed, since the effects need not occur in the same direction and to the same degree in different measurement variables. Because of the hopelessly confounded sources of error it does

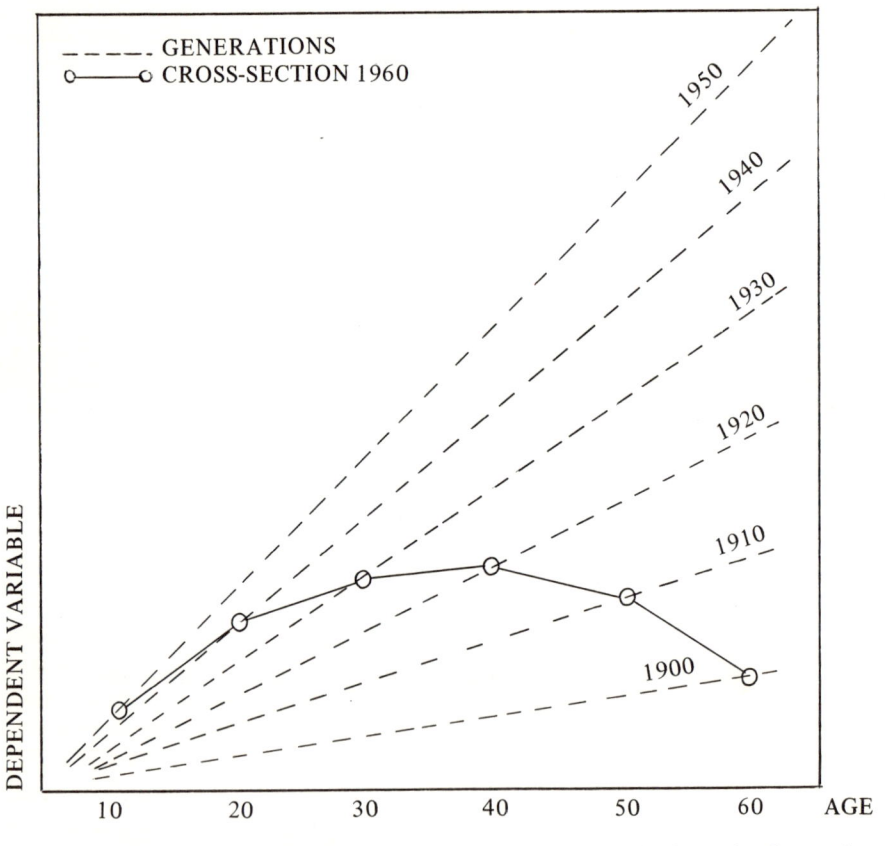

From P. B. Baltes. 1968. Longitudinal and cross-sectional sequences in the study of age and generation effects. *Human Development,* Vol. 11, used by permission of the publisher.

FIGURE 1. A hypothetical example for the effects of generation differences on the results of a cross-sectional study.

not seem feasible to make *a posteriori* statements with respect to differential validity of the results obtained by cross-sectional versus longitudinal investigations. If one considers the process of making at least one controlled comparison as the basis of securing scientific evidence (Campbell and Stanley, 1963), both conventional designs have such a total absence of control as to be of almost no scientific value. More differentiated research designs are needed to control these various deficiencies.

The above shortcomings, noted by Baltes (1968), have as a common basis the fact that different age samples (S_i, S_i^n) do not only differ with respect to age (main effect) but with respect to other factors as well (error). The various methodological deficiencies of classic developmental designs suggested by Baltes (1968), Kessen (1960), Schaie (1965, 1970), and other critics (listed previously) make it illogical to interpret sample differences as an age level main effect alone. Both classical designs produce uncontrolled sources of variance which result in a confounded error component. Uncontrolled generation (cohort) differences, as noted by Baltes and Nesselroade (1969), most decisively invalidate the assessment of long-term ontogenetic change. These differences limit the external validity (generalizability) of conventional *longitudinal* results and obscure both the internal validity (experimental treatment differences) and external validity of conventional *cross-sectional* studies.

The important point to grasp from the above material on classical developmental designs is that *neither* design provides clear-cut, unambiguous results. In fact both designs, although by far the most frequently employed models of data collection by developmentalists, are at best partially invalid. Particularly frustrating is that both developmental designs lend themselves to the following fallacious argument: differences between age groups (e.g., 10- vs. 20-year-olds) on any dependent measure (e.g., strength, vocabulary size) are the result of such an age difference (circular reasoning). An example employing such logic is as follows: Joe—10 years of age—has a larger vocabulary than John—5 years of age—because Joe is five years older. Recall from early material that age *does not* cause anything. Rather, age (as a marker within the time dimension) is a generic dependent variable defined by empirical referents. It should be obvious that many variables may correlate with a given measured attribute of an individual: e.g., sex, race, education, socioeconomic status, and prenatal environment. For example, such variables as education, socioeconomic status, and prenatal environment certainly are associated with intelligence test performance. In brief, age increments *do not* explain differences in attribute values among various age groups.

Two major and related breakthroughs have recently been made regarding the inadequacy of the classical developmental designs. These two accomplishments center on (a) *developmental design components* and (b) *multivariate data collection designs*. Both of these areas are fundamental to even an elementary awareness of the multiple issues within the field of life-span developmental psychology. The following section on developmental design components elaborates on numerous developmental model components; i.e., dimensions accounting for specific variability in given dependent variables. Since many students fear statistics (for inappropriate reasons), it is stressed now that the section on multivariate data collection designs requires no formal knowledge of elementary statistics. An attempt has been made in the multivariate section to describe the basic components of sophisticated developmental designs without introducing the student to the statistical operations of such models.

DEVELOPMENTAL DESIGN COMPONENTS

IT HAS BEEN NOTED earlier that both *cross-sectional* and *longitudinal* designs are represented by the unidimensional formula, R (response) = f (A) (function of age). That is, both designs produce an age main effect (e.g., age increments cause age-group differences) and uncontrolled sources of error. Thus, the unidimensional formula necessitates the analysis of only one effect (independent variable). As reported earlier, many variables besides age-maturation are associated with phenotypic development. Perhaps a final example will emphasize this point:

> Charles, an institutionalized mentally retarded child of 12, has a working vocabulary of twenty words. Tom, a middle-class child of 8, has a working vocabulary of seventy-five words. Since language facility is a good indicator of intellectual facility, it is obvious that Tom is brighter than Charles. What are the possible contributing factors to the difference found in vocabulary size of the boys. Age is certainly not a variable; Charles is older than Tom. The following variables may have, however, contributed solely or jointly to the result: genetics, prenatal environment, early postnatal development, education, institutionalization, socioeconomic status.

Age, then, is only one of many design components (variables associated with phenotypic development) of a multidimensional developmental model.

Schaie (1965) was the first developmental methodologist to expand Kessen's (1960) original unifactorial paradigm. According to Schaie, the expanded developmental design model included the following design components:

R = f (A, Co, T)

where:

R = response

A = chronological age

Co = dimension of generation in terms of time of birth (cohort = special population)

T = time of measurement

The design components provide a basis for classifying individuals into categories specified by A, Co, and T. Conceptualized as separate entities, the three components represent different antecedent conditions of developmental change. Schaie suggests that age (A) differences represent maturation effects, time of measurement differences (T) represent environmental effects, and cohort differences (Co) represent environmental and/or hereditary effects. It is important to note that these variables are not independent.

Baltes and Nesselroade (1969, 1970), associates of Schaie and also interested primarily in long-term and gross developmental change, selected the general or comparative developmental psychology advocated by Wapner (1964), Werner (1948), and Yerkes (1913) as a theoretical reference base for the inclusion of additional developmental design components. Yerkes, many decades ago, suggested multiple developmental design components:

> ...the term comparative psychology has come to mean the study of mind in organisms other than man.
> It seems wholly desirable...that we discard the present usage of comparative psychology and employ the term to designate the study of consciousness, behavior, or the products of behavior—no matter what the type of organism concerned—by the method of comparison...In fact, comparative psychology studies alike, for the purposes of obtaining detailed genetic descriptions, the facts of the psychology of man in the various stages of development and degrees of normality; of other animals; of plants; of minor social groups, people, and races.... We should have also patho-psychologists and ethnic psychologists just as we have, on the basis of another kind of interest, physiological psychologists (1913, pp. 580-581).

The following developmental model components are offered by Baltes and Nesselroade as supplements to (a) age, (b) cohort, and (c) time of measurement:

(d) species of organism—inclusion of both human and infrahuman organisms; species-membership categorization;

(e) culture—categorization of organisms according to cultural and/or ecological characteristics.

Thus, the expanded paradigm for a multidimensional developmental model is as follows:

R = f (A, Co, T, S, Cu)

where:

A = age (life span)

Co = cohort (generation)

T = time of measurement (specific environmental influences)

S = classes of organisms in terms of cultural or ecological characteristics.

Cu = classes of organisms in terms of cultural or ecological characteristics.

It is presently suggested that a multidimensional developmental model would prove more useful if the components or parameters noted above were further delineated. Depending on the species and/or period of the life span of interest, the following model parameters—dimensions accounting for variance components in various dependent measures—should be acknowledged: *prenatal environment, Pe; early experience, Ee; sex, Sx; race, Rc; socioeconomic status, SES; intelligence, I; role or occupation, Ro;* and *education, Ed.* These correlated, multiple design components, with possible associated research concerns, are illustrated in Figure 2.

Model components	Levels		
Age	10	20	30
Time of measurement	1970	1970	1970
Cohort	1960	1950	1940
Species	Human	Chimpanzee	Rat
Prenatal environment	Species constant	Teratogenic effects	Nutrition imbalance
Early experience	Species constant	Enriched	Deprived
Sex	Male	Female	
Culture	U.S.	U.S.S.R.	Israel
Subculture	Rural	Urban-suburb	Urban-ghetto
Race	White	Black	Indian
Socioeconomic status	Upper	Middle	Lower
Intelligence*	Normal	1 SD above	1 SD below
Role*	Professional	Skilled	Unskilled
Education*	College	High School	Grade School

*Parental or subject.

FIGURE 2. Multiple developmental design components and associated research areas.

The A, Co, and T model components are major dimensions which may be integrated with one or more minor model components. What is emphasized here is that all of the above model components have been noted as related to the development of numerous phenotypes. Obviously, a given developmental researcher deals with only a few of the model components. And, as Baltes and Nesselroade (1969) have noted, many types of restrictive subdevelopmental disciplines result from model component combinations: e.g., *species specific* (humans), *species-generation* (humans born in 1951), *species-generation-sex* (males born in 1951), etc., developmental investigations. Thus, a student of behavioral change may be specifically interested in (a) any one design component (neglecting the others), or (b) combining two or more design components. The point stressed here is that while a developmentalist may be interested in only a few model components (and levels of each), he must organize his research and conceptualizations within the complete multidimensional developmental model. Thus, if a researcher is interested in intrauterine development (Pe) of blacks and whites (Rc), he should be aware of possible confounding effects represented as error (e.g., Cu, Ed, Sx, SEC, IQ, Ro). What is emphasized here is a concern for internal and external validity of research, without which developmental construct validation is meaningless. A concern for multiple model components should rid the developmental area of such bastardly endeavors as the heredity-environment controversy. The multiple component developmental model has *at least* one pragmatic objective: students employing the multiple component model and interested in particular dimensions related to behavioral change will appreciate research and model building in other model dimensions. Although it has been pointed out many times, it is again emphasized that idol-worship in developmental psychology (e.g., behavior modification *or* cognition) restricts construct explication. It is proposed that an integrated, multidimensional developmental model will prove beneficial to both developmentalists and educational and psychological practitioners.

The contemporary controversy surrounding the findings of black-white differences on IQ tests highlights the stupidity of students of behavior who utilize a restricted developmental model (i.e., emphasizing only one model parameter). It is widely acknowledged from many investigations that blacks in general score lower on standardized IQ tests than whites in general. "Environmentalists" argue that such differences are the result of environmental factors only (e.g., standardized tests favor middle-class whites—reflect middle-class values, achievements). "Geneticists" argue that such IQ test differences are the result of hereditary factors only (e.g., whites have a different genome than blacks). The hard facts suggest that both camps have some validity in their proposals. First, however, it must be explicitly noted that any or all IQ tests *do not* completely define intelligence. An IQ is what an IQ test measures. Intelligence and IQ are not synonymous. Even if IQ tests met the assumptions of various validities (which they do not), such tests only record IQ or IQ components. The simple fact is that we are not sure what intelligence is. This is not to say, however, that a given society does not reward certain attributes or referents of intelligence. Language facility, an important referent of intelligence and heavily weighted in IQ tests, is basic to educational achievement. The most important point concerning the IQ controversy, however, is the lack of sophistication shown by both strict "environmentalists" and "geneticists" in interpreting black-white (yellow-white, etc.) differences. That is, intelligence—a loosely defined construct defined by multiple phenotypes—results from the complex interaction of genes and environment. The claim of "environmentalists" that the environment of blacks (or lower class or Indians) in general is less optimal than that of whites is too well substantiated to negate. This position, however, does not mean that group differences on standardized IQ tests are due completely to environmental factors. The phenomenon of *assortative mating* (selective breeding)—likes marrying likes—results in restricted gene pools for a given population. Thus, because blacks tend to marry blacks and whites tend to marry whites,[6] there are certain genetic differences. Genetic differences between whites and blacks are easily observable for such phenotypes as skin and hair texture. The findings of differential group genomes (genetic makeup) within a population reflect no values; i.e., one's genome is better than another's. The *relative* importance of genes and environment on IQ test performance has not been computed. What is a basic fact of nature, however, is that both genes and environment have effects on such performance. Neither factor can be discussed in a vacuum. The crucial question to raise in the IQ controversy is what pragmatic changes can be made to alleviate IQ differences among groups or individuals. Thus, when dealing with any individual who scores low on intelligence tests it is apparent that all model components discussed in Figure 2 must be recognized. That is, one or more of these components may be correlated with IQ test performance. Far too many professionals stress *either* heredity *or* environmental factors in diagnostic endeavors. The point made in the above multidimensional model is that either extreme is too restrictive.

---

6. Assortative mating is also detected within socioeconomic classes.

MULTIVARIATE DATA COLLECTION DESIGNS: DEPENDENT VARIABLES

A NUMBER OF AUTHORS have attempted to eradicate particular methodological inadequacies inherent in the classical developmental designs (Anastasi, 1958; Bell, 1953, 1954; Birren, 1959b; Wapner, 1964; Welford, 1961). These initial corrective manipulations were, however, of limited scope and value. Schaie (1965) proposed the first comprehensive alternative strategy to the conventional cross-sectional and longitudinal designs which delineated an age main effect only. Baltes (1968) reviewed Schaie's general model and suggested a second alternative to the classical designs. Finally, Schaie (1970) recently offered a rebuttal to Baltes's developmental model. Detailed discussions of these recent advancements in developmental designs may be found in chapters of Wohlwill, Nesselroade, and Schaie of *Life-span Developmental Psychology,* edited by Goulet and Baltes (1970). The multidimensional designs of both Baltes and Schaie emphasize the analysis of long-term change across the total life-span continuum. Further, they stress the unconfounding of the error components of developmental change. It is crucial to remember at this point the multidimensional model discussed in the previous section. Recall from the previous section that numerous developmental model components (e.g., sex, race) may be associated with any given phenotype (e.g., intellectual development). The multiple component model stresses that age (maturation) by itself cannot explain phenotype development. Although it is probably obvious, a major characteristic of the multiple component model is that any given component may be necessary but not sufficient in explaining the development (structure and/or process) of a given phenotype. In the present section, various data collection designs are presented which are based on the multidimensional developmental model. That is, these designs have been employed to delineate specific model component effects on phenotypic change.

TRIFACTORIAL DEVELOPMENTAL MODEL

In Schaie's (1965) trifactorial approach, the conventional cross-sectional and longitudinal methods are simply special cases of a general developmental model. As was discussed in detail earlier, the longitudinal method deals with intra-individual variability and the cross-sectional method emphasizes inter-individual variation. The third method of developmental analysis suggested by the trifactorial model is termed *time-lag*. The hypothesis underlying the time-lag design is whether there are differences in a given characteristic for samples equated on age but drawn from different cohorts (generations) measured at different times. This method has been applied before in social psychological research (see Schaie, 1965), but was not explicitly defined until included in Schaie's general model. Many of us implicitly employ a crude form of the time-lag method when we attempt to assess the possible differences in attitudes, morals, beliefs, etc., of adults living in various periods of American history. For example, what were the political attitudes of young adults during World War II as compared with those of young adults of the 1970s? Quite obviously these two young adult populations are from different cohorts or generations. Also noteworthy is that the attitudes of the two groups must have been assessed at different times of measurement; one in the 1940s, the other in the 1970s.

As was discussed earlier, Schaie's general developmental model incorporates the components of age (A), cohort (Co), and time of measurement (T). These components, crude correlates of development, result in the unifactorial developmental paradigm, Response = function of age, cohort, and time of measurement. Recall that these antecedent conditions of developmental change are independent and are defined as follows: (a) age differences represent maturation effects, (b) time of measurement differences represent environmental effects, and (c) cohort differences represent environmental and/or hereditary effects. These model components *are confounded,* however, in the classical cross-sectional, longitudinal, and time-lag designs.

Utilizing the cross-sectional method, the researcher analyzes for possible differences in a given phenotype for groups of different ages measured at the same time. If the researcher finds a significant difference among groups with the cross-sectional design, is such variability due only to maturation principles? Probably not. Any age differences detected within the cross-sectional design are confounded with cohort differences (representing environmental and/or genetic effects). Certainly there are continuous changes in the environment and culture of any society. These changes may be associated with any given cohort. Wohlwill (1969) provides the following example of model component confounding inherent within the cross-sectional method:

> ...That is, when a group of 60-year-olds is compared with a group of 20-year-olds, they differ not only in their respective ages, but they come from populations representing very different histories—e.g., present-day 60-year-olds lived through two world wars and a depression, whereas 20-year-olds had no such experience. Conversely, the former group grew up under vastly different circumstances in regard to education, technology, diffusion of knowledge through mass media, etc., than the latter. The repeated finding of substantial discrepancies between longitudinal and cross-sectional data, both for biological variables such as height and vital capacity (Damon, 1965) and psychological variables such as performance on various cognitive and psychomotor tasks (Kallmann and Jarvik, 1959; Schaie and Strother, 1968a, b) points to the important role which the cohort factor may play [p. 31].

Since the cross-sectional method confounds age effects with cohort effects, it is impossible to define age group differences as due to maturational principles alone. In other words, the cross-sectional method *does not* permit a delineation of maturational or cohort effects. Unfortunately, most developmental researchers finding age-related differences attempt to explain such differences on the basis of maturation. This is a critical error, and one that should be remembered when reviewing developmental research.

Employing the longitudinal design, the researcher analyzes for possible differences in a given phenotype for a group of subjects from the same cohort observed at different (succeeding) times of measurement. Within the longitudinal method, age differences are confounded with time of measurement (environmental) differences. Finally, within the time-lag method, time of measurement differences are confounded with cohort differences. Schaie (1970) provides the following summary statements concerning model component confounding within conventional designs:

1. The *cross-sectional* method measures *age differences* but confounds differences in maturational status with differences between generations.
2. The *longitudinal* method measures *age changes* but confounds differences in maturational status with environmental treatment effects.
3. The *time-lag* method measures *cultural change* but confounds environmental treatment effects with differences between generations [p. 487].

Schaie (1970) introduced the following sophisticated developmental designs to analyze the multiple model components and avoid component confounding:

 1. Cohort-sequential method
 2. Time-sequential method
 3. Cross-sequential method

Assuming the life span to be bounded by a seventy-year limit, the three components of Schaie's model (age, cohort, time of measurement) and the relationship among the conventional and sequential strategies are presented in Figure 3.

The total time required to measure all cohorts at all ages is simply twice the absolute life span of the population under study. From Figure 3, it can be observed that the model permits, over its total 140-year life span, eight independent longitudinal studies but only one cross-sectional study which includes members of all cohorts under investigation. In defining the relationships in the figure,

1. each column represents a cross-sectional study.
2. each row (where there are repeated measures) represents a longitudinal study.
3. each diagonal represents a time-lag study.
4. adjacent columns represent the time-sequential method.

Co								A						
1901	0	10	20	30	40	50	60	70	–	–	–	–	–	–
1911	–	0	10	20	30	40	50	60	70	–	–	–	–	–
1921	–	–	0	10	20	30	40	50	60	70	–	–	–	–
1931	–	–	–	0	10	20	30	40	50	60	70	–	–	–
1941	–	–	–	–	0	10	20	30	40	50	60	70	–	–
1951	–	–	–	–	–	0	10	20	30	40	50	60	70	–
1961	–	–	–	–	–	–	0	10	20	30	40	50	60	70
1971	–	–	–	–	–	–	–	0	10	20	30	40	50	60	70
T	1901	1911	1921	1931	1941	1951	1961	1971	1981	1991	2001	2011	2021	2031	2041

FIGURE 3. Ages of 10-year intervals for cohorts available to an investigator in 1971; Co = cohort, A = age, T = time of measurement (after Schaie, 1965)

A PRIMER FOR DEVELOPMENTAL METHODOLOGY   49

Cohort (year of birth)	Time of measurement
	'66 '67 '68 '69 '70 '71 '72 '73 '74 '75 '76 '77 '78 '79
1957	13
1958	12 13
1959	11 12 13
1960	10 11 12 13
1961	5 6 7 8 | 9 10 11 12 13 |
1962	5 6 7 | 8 9 10 11 12 | 13
1963	5 6 | 7 8 9 10 11 | 12 13
1964	5 | 6 7 8 9 10 | 11 12 13
1965	| 5 6 7 8 9 | 10 11 12 13
1966	5 6 7 8
1967	5 6 7
1968	5 6
1969	5

FIGURE 4. Schematic example of Schaie's sequential strategies. Entries represent ages corresponding to each combination of cohort and time of measurement (after Wohlwill, 1970).

5. adjacent rows represent the cohort-sequential method.
6. adjacent diagonals represent the cross-sequential method.

It should be obvious that any meaningful time interval may be employed, depending on the species and/or phenotype of interest. Since the present emphasis is on Schaie's three sequential strategies, another graphic example of the strategies is presented in Figure 4.

In Figure 4, the *time-sequential* design is represented by age entries included with the vertical parallelogram, *cohort-sequential* design is represented by age entries included within the horizontal parallelogram, and *cross-sequential* design is represented by age entries included within the square.

An important implication of Schaie's three-dimensional model is that model component unconfounding is possible if the researcher analyzes simultaneously two or more behavioral sequences; i.e., replication of conventional developmental designs. Because Schaie's sequential strategies are an important contribution to developmental methodology, each strategy will be discussed in detail.

TIME-SEQUENTIAL METHOD

This sequential strategy is the method of choice if the researcher is interested in unconfounding age effects from time of measurement (environmental) effects.

Quite simply, the time-sequential method includes replication of cross-sectional studies at N + 2 successive times of measurement. A schematic example of the time-sequential design is provided in Figure 5 with cell entries *a, b, c,* and *d*.

Following Schaie (1965), the time-sequential method is applicable whenever age samples of interest (target samples) represent measures of all ages (target samples) at all times of measurement. In Figure 5, the first two columns represent a time sequential strategy. More specifically, a *minimum* subset of target samples is represented by the subscripts *a, b, c,* and *d* in Figure 5. In this case, ages 5 and 6 are measured in 1966 (cohorts 1960 = 6-year-old, 1961 = 5-year-old) and 1967 (cohorts 1961 = 6-year-old, 1962 = 5-year-old). With the minimum 2 x 2 design (two succeeding ages—5, 6—measured at two succeeding times of measurements—1966, 1967—and thus three cohorts—1960, 1961, 1962), the following specific comparisons may be made:

	Cohorts	Ages	Time of Measurement
1.	1960-61	6 vs. 5	1966
2.	1960-61	6 vs. 6	1966, 1967
3.	1961	5 vs. 6	1966, 1967
4.	1961-62	5 vs. 5	1966, 1967
5.	1961-62	6 vs. 5	1967
6.	1960-62	6 vs. 5	1966, 1967

In terms of possible age differences (6 vs. 5), the confounding model component is cohort: it is impossible to study samples of different ages at the same time without cohort differences. The minimum case for the time-sequential method is presented in Figure 5 with the cell entries labeled *a, b, c,* and *d*. Schaie (1965)

Co					A				
1957	9	—	—	—	—	—	—	—	—
1958	8	9	—	—	—	—	—	—	—
1959	7	8	9	—	—	—	—	—	—
1960	6a	7	8	9	—	—	—	—	—
1961	5b	6c	7	8	9	—	—	—	—
1962	4	5d	6e	7g	8	9	—	—	—
1963	3	4	5f	6h	7	8	—	—	—
1964	2	3	4	5i	6j	7	8	9	—
1965	1	2	3	4	5k	6l	7	8	9
T	1966	1967	1968	1969	1970	1971	1972	1973	1974

FIGURE 5. Ages of cohorts measured at five ages with annual measurement intervals (after Schaie, 1965); Co = cohort, A = age, and T = time of measurement.

introduced the following formula definitions for measuring change over time for a minimum sequential strategy design (2 x 2):

[1] Cohort difference (Cod) = net effect of differences between older cohort (Co_j) and younger cohort (Co_i) for random samples controlled for age and time of measurement effects. Cod, then, equals net generational change from Co_i to Co_j.

[2] Time difference (Td) = net effect of differences between time of measurement N (T_k) and time of measurement N + 1 (T_l) for random samples controlled for age and cohort effects. Td, then, equals net environmental change from T_k to T_l.

[3] Age difference (Ad) = net maturational effect from age N (A_m) and age N + 1 (A_n) for random samples controlled for cohort and time of measurement effects. Ad, then, equals net maturational-organismic change from Am to An.

[4] Cross-sectional difference (CSd) = Ad + Cod.
[5] Longitudinal difference (Ld) = Ad + Td.
[6] Time-lag (cultural) difference (TLd) = Td + Cod.
[7] Ad = CSd − Cod.
[8] Cod = TLd − Td.
[9] Td = Ld − Ad.
[10] Ad = CSd − TLd − (Ld − Ad).
[11] $Ad = \dfrac{CSd - TLd + Ld}{2}$
[12] Cod = TLd − Ld − (CSd − Cod).
[13] $Cod = \dfrac{TLd - Ld + CSd}{2}$
[14] Td = Ld − CSd − (TLd − Td).
[15] $Td = \dfrac{Ld - CSd + TLd}{2}$

For the time-sequential method, substituting cell entries *a, b, c,* and *d* into formula 11 the age difference (Ad) for two levels (Am sampled at T_k − An sampled at T_l) is:

[16] $Ad = \dfrac{(b - a) - (b - d) + (b - c)}{2} = \dfrac{b + d - a - c}{2}$

The general formula for net age change is (age change from *m* to *n*, sampled at times of measurement *k* and *l*) :

[17] $Ad_G = \dfrac{T_k A_m + T_l A_m - T_k A_n - T_l A_n}{2}$

Schaie's 1970 revision of formula 17 is:

$$[18] \quad Ad_G = (1/T)\sum_{k=1}^{T} (A_n - A_m)$$

The operation for formula 18 is: "Sum the differences between two ages over all possible times of measurement and divide by the number of times of measurement over which summed (time-sequential method)" (Schaie, 1970, p. 490). An example of the minimum net age change design follows. Assume the cell entries *a, b, c,* and *d* in Figure 5 represent subject scores on a vocabulary test. Assume further the following group vocabulary performances:

	a	*b*	*c*	*d*
	$S_1 = 55$	$S_{11} = 25$	$S_{21} = 75$	$S_{31} = 30$
	$S_2 = 50$	$S_{12} = 20$	$S_{22} = 85$	$S_{32} = 25$
	$S_3 = 70$	$S_{13} = 40$	$S_{23} = 65$	$S_{33} = 45$
	$S_4 = 65$	$S_{14} = 35$	$S_{24} = 70$	$S_{34} = 50$
	$S_5 = 80$	$S_{15} = 30$	$S_{25} = 75$	$S_{35} = 35$
	$S_6 = 75$	$S_{16} = 40$	$S_{26} = 80$	$S_{36} = 55$
	$S_7 = 55$	$S_{17} = 35$	$S_{27} = 55$	$S_{37} = 40$
	$S_8 = 50$	$S_{18} = 45$	$S_{28} = 85$	$S_{38} = 25$
	$S_9 = 60$	$S_{19} = 25$	$S_{29} = 65$	$S_{39} = 50$
	$S_{10} = 65$	$S_{20} = 30$	$S_{30} = 60$	$S_{40} = 45$
mean	62.50	32.50	71.50	40.00
variance	106.94	62.50	105.83	116.67
standard deviation	10.34	7.91	10.29	10.80

S = subject
a = 6-yr.-olds born in 1960, tested in 1966 ($S_1 - S_{10}$)
b = 5-yr.-olds born in 1961, tested in 1966 ($S_{11} - S_{20}$)
c = 6 yr. olds born in 1961, tested in 1967 ($S_{21} - S_{30}$)
d = 5-yr.-olds born in 1962, tested in 1967 ($S_{31} - S_{40}$)

Substituting mean group scores into formula 16, the net age change for the above example is:

$$Ad = \frac{32.50 + 40.00 - 62.50 - 71.50}{2} = \frac{61.50}{2} = 30.75$$

Employing the cell entries *a, b, c,* and *d* of Figure 5 and substituting into formula 15, the net time-lag for this example is provided in the formula:

$$[19] \quad Td = \frac{(b-c) - (b-a) + (b-d)}{2} = \frac{a+b-c-d}{2}$$

The general formula for net time-lag difference (time of measurement *k* to *l*, sampled at ages *m* and *n*) is:

[20] $Td_G = \dfrac{T_k A_n + T_k A_m - T_l A_n - T_l A_m}{2}$

Schaie's 1970 revision of formula 20 is:

[21] $Td_G = (1/A) \sum\limits_{m=1}^{A} (T_l - T_k)$

The operation for formula 21 is: "Sum the differences between two times of measurement over all possible ages and divide by the number of ages over which summed (time-sequential method)" (Schaie, 1970, p. 490). Substituting mean group scores into formula 19, the net environmental effect for the above example is:

$$Td = \dfrac{62.50 + 32.50 - 71.50 - 40.00}{2} = \dfrac{16.50}{2} = 8.25$$

Employing the a, b, c, and d cell entries of Figure 5, the age x time-lag interaction (cohort confounded) is provided in the following formula:

[22] $Cod = \dfrac{(b-d) - (b-c) + (b-a)}{2} = \dfrac{b + c - a - d}{2}$

The general formula for net cohort difference (Cohort $_i$ measured a time $_k$ for age $_m$ versus cohort $_j$ measured a time $_l$ for age n) is as follows:

[23] $Cod_G = \dfrac{T_k A_m + T_l A_n - T_k A_n - T_l A_m}{2}$

Substituting mean group scores into formula 22, the net cohort effect for the above example is:

$$Cod = \dfrac{32.50 + 71.50 - 62.50 - 40.00}{2} = \dfrac{1.5}{2} = .75$$

As Schaie (1965) notes, the cohort change estimate (Cod = average net difference between cohorts$_{i, j}$ studied at time of measurement k for age m and time l for age n) within the time-sequential method is confounded. That is, "it is impossible to obtain members of the same cohort who retain the same age at two different times of measurement" (Schaie, 1965, p. 99). For independent sampling but *not* dependent sampling (matched group, repeated measures, or longitudinal designs), the analysis of variance statistical approach is the appropriate technique for data analyses of possible differences in the time-sequential strategy. Following Schaie (1965), Table 4 depicts the analysis of variance design components of the time-sequential design.

Employing DuBois (1965) and Kirk (1969) as references, analysis of variance designs deals with two or more population (sample) variances. Although most

TABLE 4

ANALYSIS OF VARIANCE FOR THE TIME-SEQUENTIAL DESIGN

Source of Variation	Mathematical Model Component	Degrees of Freedom
Between times (T)	α_i	T − 1
Between ages (A)	β_j	A − 1
Time x age interaction	β_{ij}	(T − 1)(A − 1)
Error	ξ_{ijk}	N − (T)(A)
Total variation	$\mu + \alpha_i + \beta_j + \alpha\beta_{ij} + \xi_{ijk}$	N − 1

readers should have at least an elementary knowledge of univariate analysis of variance, it is probably worthwhile to list the DuBois (pp. 358-359) summary of distinctive features in discussions of analysis of variance:

1. The insistence that the primary objective of statistical analysis is to make inferences about the population—inferences that have general validity—rather than merely the description of a particular sample.
2. The use of a precise mathematical model in the form of the exact distribution of a key statistic that would be expected by random sampling if a given null hypothesis were true. This involves careful attention to the degrees of freedom, since with the samples that are characteristic of much experimental work, the shapes of certain chance distributions (notably t and F) change markedly with variations in the degrees of freedom.
3. The development of precise hypotheses that can be tested by collecting observations. The null hypothesis can be developed in a wide variety of forms, but it is always exact, and potentially it can always be refuted (not absolutely, but at a given level of significance). Among its more useful forms are "no experimental effect" or "no difference among means," but forms that include posited parameters other than zero can be readily established.
4. The use of fixed levels in judging significance. With the normal distribution, it is mechanically simple to evaluate the rarity of an event without regard to a fixed level, such as the 5 percent level or the 1 percent level. With F (as with t), complete tables would be cumbersome, since each change in the degrees of freedom involves a new distribution. The advantage of fixed levels, however, is not merely mechanical. By deciding on a fixed level of significance in advance, standards for rejecting null hypotheses become objective for the course of the experiment, and interpretations of outcomes are less likely to be influenced by subjective considerations.
5. The use of methods to control extraneous variation that might obscure results. These include eliminating variables and sources of variation, matching subjects to form equivalent samples, and using chance

procedures, particularly tables of random numbers, to make assignments to groups.
6. Systematic designing of the experiment in advance, so that the maximum amount of useful information can be extracted from the observations.

From Table 4 and the earlier presentation of variance components, it is obvious that the two-treatment time-sequential design fits the mathematical model, $X_{ijk} = \mu + \alpha_i + \beta_j + \alpha\beta_{ij} + \xi_{ijk}$, where:

X_{ijk} = individual score

μ = population mean

α_i = treatment effect (T)

β_j = treatment effect (A)

$\alpha\beta_{ij}$ = T x A intcraction

ξ_{ijk} = error effect

In the time-sequential design, (a) increasing the number of ages measured at each time of measurement extends the age range for time-lag difference evaluation (A − 1) and (b) increasing the number of times of measurement increases degrees of freedom (T − 1). As stated earlier, the time-sequential design is the appropriate sequential technique for differentiating *aging* (A) from time-lag or time of measurement (T) effects. Also recall that Schaie interprets the age differences as representing maturation effects and the time of measurement differences as representing environmental effects. Note that the time-sequential design confounds cohort differences "since we cannot study individuals of different ages at the same time of measurement unless they also belong to different generations" (Schaie, 1970, pp. 488-489). Schaie's (1965, p. 99) summary of the time-sequential design succinctly depicts the assets and liabilities of the technique:

> Two measurements of every cohort will suffice to permit the evaluation of time-lag at all ages of interest to the investigator. It would seem, therefore, that this method should be favored whenever generalizability of a construct over time is at issue. Note that the time-sequential model controls age differences for cultural shift and time-lag differences for the effect of age. It is impossible, however, to identify an unconfounded cohort difference component. This means that the *time-sequential method will yield unambiguous results only when the assumption is met that*

The material quoted above and elsewhere in this book from K. W. Schaie. "A general model for the study of developmental problems." *Psychological Bulletin* vol. 64, 1965, pp. 92-107, © 1965 by the American Psychological Association, is reproduced by permission of the author and the copyright holder.

change in the variable under study is unrelated to genetic or cohort-specific environmental changes. This assumption is a hazardous one only when physical attributes are involved or when behaviors are studied which are thought to be affected by gross environmental crises such as wars or severe depressions. The assumption would seem to be quite tenable for many variables in the areas of ability, personality, learning, interests, and, in fact, in most matters of concern to the developmental psychologist.

If neither of the assumptions underlying the time-sequential or cohort-sequential model can be met, then recourse must be taken to another sequential model.

COHORT-SEQUENTIAL METHOD

This sequential strategy is the method of choice if the researcher is interested in differentiating cohort (generation) and maturation effects. The cohort-sequential strategy is a general case of the longitudinal design (requires longitudinal sequences for at least two cohorts studied simultaneously) and is depicted in the last two rows of Figure 5. The entries labeled *i, j, k,* and *l* in Figure 5 represent the minimum set of target samples for this sequential method. In this case, age 5 (cohort 1964) is measured on some dependent variable at time of measurement 1969, and ages 5 (cohort 1965) and 6 (cohort 1964) are tested at time of measurement 1970, and age 6 (cohort 1965) is tested at time of measurement 1971. With the minimum 2 x 2 design (cohorts—1964, 1965—ages—5, 6—and thus studied at three times of measurement—1969, 1970, 1971) the following specific comparisons may be made:

	Cohorts	Ages	Time of Measurement
1.	1964-65	5 vs. 5	1969, 1970
2.	1964-65	6 vs. 6	1970, 1971
3.	1964	5 vs. 6	1969, 1970
4.	1965	5 vs. 6	1970, 1971
5.	1964-65	5 vs. 6	1970
6.	1964-65	5 vs. 6	1969, 1971

Since it is impossible to study all ages for all cohorts at identical times of measurement, the model component confound in the time-sequential design is time of measurement (environment). Schaie (1965) introduced the following formula-definitions for measuring change over cohorts for a minimum sequential strategy design (2 x 2):

Utilizing the entries *i, j, k,* and *l* in Figure 5 and substituting them into formula 11, the net age change over one unit of time at age 5 (or A_m sampled at T_k − A_n sampled at T_l) is:

A PRIMER FOR DEVELOPMENTAL METHODOLOGY

[24] $\quad Ad = \dfrac{(k-j) - (k-i) + (k-l)}{2} = \dfrac{i - j + k - l}{2}$

The general formula for net age change (age change m to n, sampled for cohorts i and j) is:

[25] $\quad Ad_G = \dfrac{Co_i A_m - Co_i A_n + Co_j A_m - Co_j A_n)}{2}$

Schaie's 1970 revision of formula 25 is:

[26] $\quad Ad_G = (1/Co) \sum\limits_{i=1}^{Co} (A_n - A_m)$

The operation for formula 26 is: "Sum the differences between two ages over all possible cohorts and divide by the number of cohorts over which summed (cohort-sequential method)" (Schaie, 1970, p. 489).

An example of the minimum net age change cohort-sequential design is as follows: Assume that entries i, j, k, and l represent subject scores on a vocabulary test. Assume further that the vocabulary group performances for entries are as follows:

		Mean Score
i =	5-yr.-olds born in 1964, tested in 1969	32.50
j =	6-yr.-olds born in 1964, tested in 1970	62.50
k =	5-yr.-olds born in 1965, tested in 1970	40.00
l =	6-yr.-olds born in 1965, tested in 1971	71.50

Substituting mean group scores into formula 25, the net age change for the above example is:

$$Ad = \dfrac{32.50 - 62.50 + 40.00 - 71.50}{2} = \dfrac{61.50}{2} = 30.75$$

Employing cell entries i, j, k, and l and substituting into formula 13 the net cohort difference between Co_i (1964) and Co_j (1965) is provided in the formula:

[27] $\quad Cod = \dfrac{(k-i) - (k-l) + (k-j)}{2} = \dfrac{k + l - i - j}{2}$

The general formula for net cohort change (between cohorts i and j for ages at time of measurement m and n) is:

[28] $\quad Cod_G = \dfrac{Co_j A_m + Co_j A_n - Co_i A_m - Co_i A_n}{2}$

Schaie's 1970 revision of formula 28 is:

$$[29] \quad Cod_G = (1/A) \sum_{m=1}^{A} (Co_j - Co_i)$$

The operation for formula 29 is: "Sum the differences between two cohorts over all possible ages and divide by the number of ages over which summed (cohort-sequential method)" (Schaie, 1970, p. 490).

Substituting mean group scores into formula 27, the net cohort effect for the example is:

$$Cod = \frac{40.00 + 71.50 - 32.50 - 61.50}{2} = \frac{16.50}{2} = 8.25$$

The age x cohort interaction (time of measurement confound) is provided in the following formula (substituting i, j, k, l entries into formula 15):

$$[30] \quad Td = \frac{(k-l) - (k-j) + (k-i)}{2} = \frac{j + k - i - l}{2}$$

The general formula for the average net cohort change (Co_i at A_m and Co_j at A_n) is:

$$[31] \quad Td_G = \frac{Co_i A_n + Co_j A_m - Co_i A_n - Co_j A_m}{2}$$

Substituting mean group scores for the $i, j, k,$ and l entry samples the average net time of measurement change (Co_i at A_m vs. Co_j at A_n) is:

$$Td = \frac{62.50 + 40.00 - 32.50 - 71.50}{2} = \frac{1.50}{2} = .75$$

Again, note that the model component confound in the cohort-sequential method is time of measurement (environment), i.e., impossible to study all ages for all cohorts at identical times of measurement. Schaie (1970, p. 488) presents the following regarding the cohort x age interaction: "... a significant cohort x age interaction could denote either that age changes occur at different rates for different cohorts or that there is a time of measurement confound."

For independent sampling, the analysis of variance is the appropriate technique for data analysis for significance testing of net differences in the cohort-sequential method. Following Schaie (1965) Table 5 depicts the analysis of variance design components of this sequential strategy.

As with the time-sequential method, the minimum 2 x 2 cohort sequential design fits the mathematical model $X_{ijk} = \mu + \alpha_i + \beta_j + \alpha\beta_{ij} + \Sigma_{ijk}$, where:

X_{ijk} = individual score

TABLE 5
ANALYSIS OF VARIANCE FOR THE COHORT-SEQUENTIAL DESIGN

Source of Variation	Mathematical Model Component	Degrees of Freedom
Between cohorts (Co)	α_i	Co - 1
Between ages (A)	β_j	A - 1
Cohort x age interaction	$\alpha\beta_{ij}$	(Co - 1)(A - 1)
Error	ξ_{ijk}	N^a - (Co)(A)
Total variation	$\mu + \alpha_i + \beta_j + \alpha\beta_{ijk} + \xi_{ijk}$	N - 1

a = Number of observations

μ = population mean
α_i = treatment effect (Co)
β_j = treatment effect (A)
$\alpha\beta_{ij}$ = Co x A interaction
ξ_{ijk} = error effect

For the cohort sequential design, (a) "increasing the number of successive times of measurement for all cohorts will extend the age range for which cohort differences can be evaluated, while [b] increasing the number of sequences would augment the number of cohorts over which age differences can be generalized" (Schaie, 1965, p. 98).

For dependent sampling or repeated measures techniques, Table 6 depicts the analysis of variance design components of the cohort-sequential design (after Schaie, 1965).

Detailed assumptions and restrictions of repeated measures designs, as well as computational formulas for the minimum 2 x 2 design, are presented in Kirk (1969). Following Kirk (1969, p. 252), the mathematical model components of Table 6 are defined as follows:

X_{ijk} = score for randomly selected entry (k) in treatment population ab_{ij} (a = level of α_i; b = level of β_j);
μ = grand mean of treatment levels;
α_i = treatment effect $_i$ (Co), constant for all entries within treatment population $_i$;
β_j = treatment effect $_j$ (A), constant for all entries within treatment population $_j$;
$\pi k_{(i)}$ = constant associated with entry $_k$, nested under α_i level (Subjects within groups error term);

TABLE 6

REPEATED MEASURES ANALYSIS OF VARIANCE FOR THE COHORT-SEQUENTIAL DESIGN

Source of Variation	Mathematical Model Component	Degrees of Freedom
Between subjects		$\frac{N}{A} - 1$
Between cohorts (Co)	α_i	$Co - 1$
Error (between subjects)	$\pi_{k(i)}$	$\frac{N}{A} - Co$
Within subjects		$N - \frac{N}{A}$
Between ages (A)	β_j	$A - 1$
Cohort x age interaction	$\alpha\beta_{ij}$	$(Co - 1)(A - 1)$
Error (within subjects)	$\beta\pi_{jk(i)}$	$N - (\frac{N}{A}) - Co(A - 1)$
Total variation	$X_{ijk} = \mu + \alpha_i + \pi_{k(i)} + \beta_j +$ $\alpha\beta_{ij} + \beta\pi_{jk(i)} + \xi_{ijk}$	$N - 1$

$\alpha\beta_{ij}$ = effect that represents nonadditivity of α_i and β_j effects (Co x A interaction);

$\beta\pi_{jk(i)}$ = effect that represents nonadditivity of β_j and $\pi_{k(i)}$ effects (A x subjects within groups error term);

$\xi_{(ijk)}$ = experimental error term, independent of $\pi_{k(i)}$ and $\beta\pi_{jk(i)}$ error terms; in this mixed linear model, $\xi_{(ijk)}$ cannot be estimated separately from $\beta\pi_{jk(i)}$.

As is suggested by the terms dependent sampling and repeated measures, a major characteristic of repeated measures designs is that the subject serves as his own control—"responses of individual subjects to the treatments are measured in terms of deviations about a point which measures the average responsiveness of that individual subject. Hence variability due to differences in the average responsiveness of the subjects is eliminated from the experimental error (if an additive model is appropriate)" (Winer, 1962, p. 105). Kessen's (page 26 of this text) developmental hypothetical data, Wohlwill's (page 30 of this text) discussion of three types of information preserved in longitudinal designs, and Baltes's (page 35 of this text) discussion of specific methodological shortcomings associated with developmental designs provide the reader with major characteristics of repeated measures designs.

Although the reader is referred to Schaie (1965) for a more complete presentation relating to characteristics of the repeated measures cohort-sequential design, the following statements should provide an introduction to such design assets and liabilities.

[1] Whenever experimental error is large or where differences between experimental conditions, though significant and stable, are expected to be small, variability may be reduced markedly by use of the matched group design. [See Kessen's example, page 26 of this text.]

[2] In a repeated measurement design the investigator obtains measures on the same sample of subjects at different times. Such repetition poses no problems where physical attributes are involved, but complications arise whenever variables are studied which are amenable to practice or where the testing procedure effects the behavior to be measured. [See Baltes's discussion of specific methodological shortcomings associated with developmental designs, page 35 of this text.]

[3] Instead of comparing independently derived groups of subjects and being limited thereby to statements of the difference between group means, the repeated measurement design permits comparing each observation of a subject's behavior with some earlier or later measurements.... [See Wohlwill's discussion of three types of information preserved in longitudinal designs, page 30 of this text.]

[4] In theory, therefore, it should be possible to detect small but reliable changes because the matching procedure will result in more sensitive estimates of such changes.

[5] Unless adequate controls are provided, and these are for practical and understandable reasons usually lacking in developmental studies, the small but significant changes may simply be a function of practice or other artifacts....

[6] It is virtually impossible to maintain a single sample in its entirety over any length of time. Unfortunately, sampling attrition is not random but is often related to the very variables being studied. [See Baltes's discussion of specific methodological shortcomings associated with developmental designs, page 35 of this text.] Unless it can be shown that the reduced sample for which repeated measurements are available is substantially similar to the original sample, it is, of course, not possible to generalize even for the single cohort sampled. No such evidence is readily available for most of the various longitudinal studies reported in the literature.

[7] Attention should further be called to the fact that for an equal number of observations the degrees of freedom available for the error term used to test mean differences will always be less for the replicated than for independently derived measurements. The gain in sensitivity must, therefore, exceed the loss caused by testing a smaller number of individuals before the repeated measurement design will pay off.

[8]   The repeated measurement design will always be inferior to the independent sample design in evaluating cohort differences, since such differences must of necessity involve the comparison of independent samples. . . .

[9]   . . . the repeated measurement designs will become efficient only where measures have high reliability or where measures are taken at many ages or many times.

[10] . . . The age difference and age x cohort-interaction terms in the cohort sequential repeated measurement design will be confounded both with time differences and practice effects.

[11] . . . it is impossible to separate age differences from practice effects in the cohort-sequential model [pp. 104-105]. [A detailed presentation of a direct estimate of practice effects in a repeated measures cohort-sequential design is presented in Schaie (1965).]

Again, Schaie's (1965, p. 98) summary of the cohort-sequential design succinctly depicts the assets and liabilities of the technique.

> The cohort-sequential design is clearly the method of choice when a test of the generalizability of constructs over different generations (cohorts) is required. It will be noted that this design controls for cohort differences which might be attributable to genetic changes at all ages and that the cohort differences are controlled for age differences. But it is not possible in this design to identify an unconfounded time difference component. This means that the cohort-sequential method will yield unambiguous results only when the assumption is met that changes in the variable under study are unrelated to cultural change. This assumption is rarely met except in the study of physical attributes or in investigations involving infrahuman organisms. Even when this assumption is met, it is as difficult to obtain an ample coverage of the life span of the organism in this variant as in the single-cohort or repeated measurement longitudinal design. Moreover, it will be seen that the cohort-sequential method will provide no more accurate estimates of age differences than do the more efficient alternative procedures.

CROSS-SEQUENTIAL METHOD

The final sequential strategy proposed by Schaie is the method of choice if the researcher is interested in differentiating cohort (generation) from time of measurement effects. The cross-sequential strategy is the general case of the time-lag method (requires examination of two or more samples from the same cohort at two or more times of measurement), and is depicted by rows 6 and 7 of Figure 5. The entries labeled e, f, g, and h in Figure 5 represent the minimum set of target samples for this sequential method. In this case, ages 5 (cohort 1963) and 6 (cohort 1962) are measured on some dependent variable at time of measurement 1968, and ages 6 (cohort 1963) and 7 (cohort 1962) are tested at time of measurement 1969. With the minimum 2 x 2 design (cohorts—1962, 1963, measured at two succeeding times of measurement—1968, 1969, and thus three ages—5, 6, 7), the following specific comparisons may be made:

	Cohorts	Ages	Time of Measurement
1.	1962-63	6 vs. 5	1968
2.	1962-63	6 vs. 6	1968, 1969
3.	1962	6 vs. 7	1968, 1969
4.	1963	5 vs. 6	1968, 1969
5.	1962-63	6 vs. 7	1969
6.	1962-63	5 vs. 7	1968, 1969

Since the cross-sequential design includes measures of two or more samples from the same cohort at two or more times of measurement, age is the confounded model component; i.e., members of different cohorts also differ in age at any time of measurement. This sequential strategy involves replicating studies of two or more cohorts at two or more times of measurement. Schaie (1965) introduced the following formula-definitions for differentiating cohort and time of measurement effects (the age effect is assumed to be absent) for the minimum 2 x 2 sequential strategy:

Utilizing the entries e, f, g, and h in Figure 5 and substituting them into formula 13, the net cohort change between cohorts i and j (1962, 1963) studied at times of measurement k and l (1968, 1969) is:

[31] $\text{Cod} = \dfrac{(e-h)-(e-g)+(e-f)}{2} = \dfrac{e+g-f-h}{2}$

The general formula for net cohort change (difference between Co_i and Co_j sampled at T_k and T_l) is:

[32] $\text{Cod}_G = \dfrac{Co_i\,T_k + Co_i\,T_l - Co_j\,T_k - Co_j\,T_l}{2}$

Schaie's 1970 revision of formula 32 is:

[33] $\text{Cod}_G = (1/T) \sum\limits_{k=1}^{T} (Co_j - Co_i)$

The operation for formula 33 is: "Sum the differences between two cohorts over all possible times of measurement and divide by the number of times of measurement over which summed (cross-sequential method)" (Schaie, 1970, p. 490).

An example of the minimum net cohort change cross-sequential design is as follows: Assume that entries *e, f, g,* and *h* represent subject scores on a vocabulary test. Assume further that the vocabulary group performances for entries are as follows:

	Mean Score
e = 6-year-olds born in 1962, tested in 1968	40.00
f = 5-year-olds born in 1963, tested in 1968	32.50
g = 7-year-olds born in 1962, tested in 1969	71.50
h = 6-year-olds born in 1963, tested in 1969	62.50

Substituting mean group scores for *e, f, g,* and *h* entry examples into formula 31, the net cohort difference on the vocabulary variable (1962, 1963 cohorts tested in 1968, 1969) is:

$$\text{Cod} = \frac{40.00 + 71.50 - 32.50 - 62.50}{2} = \frac{16.50}{2} = 8.25$$

Utilizing the *e, f, g,* and *h* entry subscripts and substituting into formula 15, the net time-lag for cohorts 1963 and 1964 sampled at time of measurement 1968 and 1969 is:

[34] $$\text{Td} = \frac{(e-g) - (e-f) + (e-h)}{2} = \frac{e + f - g - h}{2}$$

The general formula for the net cultural or environmental change (Co_i and Co_j sampled at T_k and T_l) is:

[35] $$\text{Td}_G = \frac{Co_i T_k + Co_j T_k - Co_i T_l - Co_j T_l}{2}$$

Schaie's 1970 revision of formula 35 is:

[36] $$\text{Td}_G = (1/Co) \sum_{i=1}^{Co} (T_l - T_k)$$

The operation for formula 36 is: "Sum the differences between two times of measurement over all possible cohorts and divide by the number of cohorts over which summed (cross-sequential method)" (Schaie, 1970, p. 490).

Substituting mean group scores into formula 34, the net time of measurement difference for the example is:

$$\text{Td} = \frac{40.00 + 32.50 - 71.50 - 62.50}{2} = \frac{61.50}{2} = 30.75$$

The cohort x time of measurement interaction (age confounded) is estimated in the following formula (substituting entries *e, f, g,* and *h* into formula 11):

[37] $Ad = \dfrac{(e-f) - (e-h) + (e-g)}{2} = \dfrac{e + h - f - g}{2}$

The general formula for the average net age change for the one year time interval and one year age unit (Co_i at T_k and Co_j at T_l) is:

[38] $Ad_G = \dfrac{Co_i\, T_k + Co_j\, T_l - Co_j\, T_k - Co_i\, T_l}{2}$

Substituting mean group scores for e, f, g, and h entry examples into formula 37, the cohort x time of measurement interaction estimate for cohorts 1962 and 1963 tested at time of measurement 1968 and 1969 is:

$Ad = \dfrac{40.00 + 62.50 - 32.50 - 71.50}{2} = \dfrac{1.50}{2} = .75$

For independent sampling, the analysis of variance is again the appropriate technique for data analysis for significance testing of net differences in the cross-sequential method. Following Schaie (1965), Table 7 depicts the analysis of variance design components of this sequential strategy.

As with the preceding sequential methods, the minimum 2 x 2 cross-sequential design fits the linear mathematical model $X_{ijk} = \mu + \alpha_i + \beta_j + \alpha\beta_{ij} + \xi_{ijk}$, where:

X_{ijk} = individual score

μ = population mean

α_i = treatment effect (Co)

β_j = treatment effect (T)

$\alpha\beta_{ij}$ = Co x T interaction

ξ_{ijk} = error effect

For the cross-sequential design, (a) "Adding to the number of cohorts in this design will increase the range over which time differences can be generalized, while [b] augmenting the number of times of measurement will permit generalization over time for cohort differences" (Schaie, 1965, p. 100). Further, expanding over rows and columns (see Figure 5) will increase the external validity (generalization) of the cohort x time of measurement (age confounded) interaction.

For dependent sampling or repeated measures techniques, Table 8 depicts the analysis of variance design components of the cross-sequential design (after Schaie, 1965).

Following Kirk (1969) the mathematical model components of Table 8 are defined as follows:

TABLE 7
ANALYSIS OF VARIANCE FOR THE CROSS-SEQUENTIAL DESIGN

Source of Variation	Mathematical Model Component	Degrees of Freedom
Between cohorts (Co)	α_i	Co - 1
Between times (T)	β_j	T - 1
Cohort x time interaction	$\alpha\beta_{ij}$	(Co - 1)(T - 1)
Error	ξ_{ijk}	N - (Co)(T)
Total variation	$\mu + \alpha_i + \beta_j + \alpha\beta_{ij} + \xi_{ijk}$	N - 1

X_{ijk} = score for randomly selected entry (k) in treatment population ab_{ij} (a = level of α_i; b = level of β_j);

μ = grand mean of treatment levels;

α_i = treatment effect $_i$ (Co), constant for all entries within treatment population $_i$;

β_j = treatment effect $_j$ (T), constant for all entries within treatment population $_j$;

$\pi_{k(i)}$ = constant associated with entry $_k$, nested under α_i level (subjects within groups error term);

$\beta\pi_{jk(i)}$ = effect that represents nonadditivity of β_j and $\pi_{k(i)}$ effects (T x subjects within groups error term);

$\alpha\beta_{ij}$ = effect that represents nonadditivity of α_i and β_j effects (Co x T interaction);

$\xi_{(ijk)}$ = experimental error term, independent of $\pi_{k(i)}$ and $\beta\pi_{jk(i)}$ error terms; in this mixed linear model, $\xi_{(ijk)}$ cannot be estimated separately from $\beta\pi_{jk(i)}$.

The reader is referred to Schaie (1965) for a complete discussion delineating characteristics of the cross-sequential design. The first ten statements characteristic of repeated measures designs (pages 61-62) may also be included within the cross-sequential design. Two other statements are characteristic of this sequential design:

1. . . . in the cross-sequential repeated measurement design, the time-difference and cohort-time interactions will be confounded with age differences and practice effects.
2. . . . it is impossible to separate time differences from practice effects in cross-sequential model [Schaie, 1965, p. 105].

TABLE 8

REPEATED MEASURES ANALYSIS OF VARIANCE
FOR THE CROSS-SEQUENTIAL DESIGN

Source of Variation	Mathematical Model Components	Degrees of Freedom
Between subjects		$\frac{N}{T} - 1$
Between cohorts (Co)	α_i	$Co - 1$
Error (between subjects)	$\pi_{k(i)}$	$\frac{N}{T} - Co$
Within subjects		$N - \frac{N}{T}$
Between times (T)	β_j	$T - 1$
Cohort x time interaction	$\alpha\beta_{ij}$	$(Co - 1)(T - 1)$
Error (within subjects)	$\beta\pi_{jk(i)}$	$N - (\frac{N}{T}) - Co(T - 1)$
Total variation	$X_{ijk} = \mu + \alpha_i + \beta_j +$ $\alpha\beta_{ij} + \beta\pi_{jk(i)} + \xi_{ijk}$	$N - 1$

In summarizing the cross-sequential strategy, Schaie (1965), again, offers a succinct analysis:

> The cross-sequential model controls time differences for changes over generations and cohort differences for cultural shift. No unconfounded age difference component is available in this model, and consequently it follows that time-lag methods will yield unambiguous results only when the assumption is met that change in the variable under study is unrelated to age changes. This assumption may be tenable for many characteristics which remain stable over substantial portions of the organism's life span. It is not usually supported in developmental studies of childhood but may frequently apply to investigations involving behavior change over time in adults. It should be noted that the cross-sequential model can be applied to any research design employing either the cohort or time-sequential methods by simply adding one more sample as indicated in the upper triangle in [Figure 5].

In concluding this discussion of Schaie's tri-dimensional developmental model, a number of summary statements are noted (based on Schaie, 1965, 1970; Baltes, 1968; and Wohlwill, 1970).

1. The multiple developmental model (see Figure 2) depicts development of any phenotype as a result of more than one model component. At the very

least, such a model introduces the possibility that numerous model components may be associated with phenotypic development (structure and process).

2. It follows from *1* that age (maturation) alone cannot explain phenotypic development.

3. From *1* and *2*, it is argued that sophisticated designs are required to measure the effects of multiple model components with a minimum of component confounding.

4. Classical developmental designs (cross-sectional and longitudinal) have inherent methodological flaws, producing an age main effect and confounded sources of error. See page 31 of this text for further discussion of this problem for developmentalists and experimentalists (interested in developmental issues). It is worthwhile to point out the probable predicament that will be faced by experimentalists wishing to enter the developmental arena. If the behavioral journals of the 1970s are any indication, classic experimentalists are dabbling in developmental issues at a rapid rate. Unfortunately, these experimentalists are employing the comparative—cross-sectional—design that has been criticized as being inadequate. Thus, experimentalists who introduce age or sex or socioeconomic status or race, etc., as variables in their experimental designs are dealing with an age or sex or socioeconomic status or race, etc., main effect and confounded sources of variability. The point made here is that experimentalists need to understand developmental model components, inadequacies (and assets) of classical developmental designs, and sophisticated developmental methods if they are to effectively deal with developmental issues.

5. Schaie's sequential strategies stem, in part, from Kessen's $R = f(A, P)$, $R = f(A, S)$, and $R = f(A, P, S)$ research paradigms. Such research paradigms do not, however, deal with the unconfounding of age, cohort, and time of measurement model components.

6. Schaie reintroduced the time-lag developmental design: $cohort_i$, age_m, time of $measurement_k$ vs. $cohort_j$, age_m, time of $measurement_l$.

7. Schaie's three model components are not independent. Such dependency requires selection of sequential strategies for model component unconfounding; separate and/or combinatorial analysis. Age differences are proposed to represent maturational effects. Note from the introductory chapter that age (as a referent of time) causes nothing. Developmentalists employ age as a referent or generic dependent variable of maturational principles. Time of measurement differences are proposed to represent environmental effects. Finally, cohort differences are proposed to represent environmental and/or genetic effects. Differentiating between genetic, environmental, or a combination effect when dealing with a cohort effect is a clinical one.

8. The cohort-sequential method, most general case of the classical longitudinal design, is the method of choice in differentiating cohort effects

from maturational effects. The minimum case of the cohort-sequential design incorporates two cohorts (Co_i, Co_j), studied at two age levels (A_m, A_n) and thus at three times of measurement (T_k, T_l, T_m). Time of measurement is the developmental model component which is confounded.

9. The time-sequential method, most general case of the classical cross-sectional design, is the method of choice in differentiating maturational effects from time of measurement or environmental effects. The minimum case of the time-sequential design incorporates samples of two age levels (A_m, A_n), at two times of measurement (T_k, T_l), from three cohorts (Co_i, Co_j, Co_k). Cohort is the developmental model component which is confounded.

10. The cross-sequential method, most general case of the time-lag design, is the method of choice in differentiating time of measurement effects from cohort effects. The minimum case of the cross-sequential design incorporates two age level samples from the same cohort (Co_i, Co_j) (A_n, A_o for Co_i; A_m, A_n for Co_j) at two times of measurement (T_k, T_l). Age is the developmental model component which is confounded.

11. All three sequential strategies fit the linear mathematical model, $X_{ijk} = \mu + \alpha_i + \beta_j + \alpha\beta_{ij} + \xi_{ijk}$ for independent sampling. Utilizing this two factor model, it is possible to test for model component main effects (α_i, β_j) and simple effects (interaction, $\alpha\beta_{ij}$).

12. For the cohort-sequential and cross-sequential strategies only, it is possible to employ repeated measures designs. It is not possible to utilize a repeated measures design for the time-sequential method because dependent sampling is not possible for the first or last cohort included within a sequential cross-sectional design (see Figure 5).

13. Schaie notes that a possible practice effect is confounded within cohort- and cross-sequential repeated measures strategies, unless (a) age is not a significant effect in the cohort-sequential design (A, Co x A) and (b) time of measurement is not a significant effect in the cross-sequential strategy (T, Co x T).

14. Possible practice effects may be clearly and independently estimated within the cohort- and cross-sequential strategies if dependent measures of independent random samples are compared with isomorphic sequential design repeated measures.

15. Although all three sequential strategies may be appropriate in analyzing for phenotypic change in short-lived organisms, Schaie notes that only the time- and cross-sequential designs are feasible in analyzing for human phenotypic change. Schaie's rejection of the time-sequential design for long-term human research has been stated previously. In brief, such a rejection is based on the fact that the inherent assumption underlying the time-sequential method—changes in the dependent variable studied are unrelated to cultural change—is infrequently

met in human research. It is again noted that the design is appropriate for short-term human research, and research on physical attributes (where time of measurement effects may be minimal, i.e., nonsignificant).

16. Although examples of the three sequential strategies were given within a 2 x 2 factorial, remember that this is the minimal case of any sequential strategy. For the cohort-sequential design the researcher is able to study all target cohorts (total number of cohorts in the design) at all target ages (total age units in the design) with time of measurement confounded. For the cross-sequential strategy, the researcher is able to study all target cohorts at all target times of measurement (total measurement units in the design) with age confounded. Finally, for the time sequential method, the researcher is able to study all target ages at all target times of measurement with cohort confounded.

In concluding Schaie's advances in developmental designs, it is appropriate to quote from this methodologist again in relation to the most efficient research strategy available to the developmentalist employing sequential designs:

> 1. Draw a random sample from each cohort over the age range to be investigated, and measure at Time k (Score A).
> 2. Get a second measurement on all subjects tested at Time k at Time l (Score B).
> 3. Draw a new random sample from each cohort in the range tested at Time k plus one cohort below that range, and test at Time l (Score C).
>
> The following comparisons may now be made: (a) Cross-sequential model (Scores A and C), (b) Time-sequential (Scores A and C), (c) Cross-sequential model with repeated measurements (Scores A and B), (d) Cross-sectional model, controlling for effect of practice (Scores B and C).
>
> Almost all questions of interest to the developmental researcher can be handled by this strategy, which should yield interpretable results in practically all empirical situations.* Sampling attrition in the repeated measurement part of the study should be fairly limited over a single time interval. Also, if desired, the new random sample obtained at Time l will provide the base for a second repeated measurement study, and any cohort or cohort sequence can, of course, be followed further if a conventional longitudinal study is to be pursued (Schaie 1965, p. 107).

BIFACTORIAL DEVELOPMENTAL MODEL

As mentioned at the beginning of this chapter, Baltes (1968) was critical of Schaie's trifactorial (age, cohort, time of measurement) general developmental model. Because of apparent inadequacies associated with the formal definition and interpretation of the three design components, Baltes reduced the tridimen-

---

* The proposed research strategy has been applied to the study of developmental changes in adult cognitive behavior (Schaie and Strother, 1964a, 1964b).

sional model into a bidimensional model consisting of design components age and cohort only:

R = f (A, Co), where:
R = dependent variable (e.g., height)
A = age
Co = cohort or generation

It is mathematically possible (Baltes and Nesselroade, 1969) to consider the remaining *combinations* of the three general developmental model components: R = f (A, T) and R = f (Co, T). Baltes suggests that (a) the design components should be descriptive and not explanatory, and (b) Schaie's introduction of a third design component is redundant. The design components display the following formal relationships: A = T − Co, T = A + Co, and Co = T − A. These relationships result from the fact that after two components have been defined, the remaining component is fixed. Baltes (1968, p. 157) notes that since the three developmental components are interdependent, not independent, "the three components do not satisfy the qualifications of three true experimental variables, namely they cannot be defined and varied independently."

Baltes's A and Co components in his bidimensional model are regarded as descriptive concepts only; no attempt was made to give them differential explanatory meaning as Schaie had previously suggested in his general model (Baltes, 1968). The age and cohort components refer only to the fact that individuals can be assigned to specific age levels and generations. Baltes's bidimensional model can be transformed into an experimental analysis of variance design (similar to Schaie's model) employing *repeated* and/or *independent* measurements with respect to the age factor (see Baltes, 1968; Baltes and Nesselroade, 1969, 1970). The age and cohort components represent fixed factors in the bidimensional analysis of variance design (where number of age and cohort groups employed is identical with the number of factorial levels respectively). A 2 x 2 factorial is the minimum design which can be derived from Baltes's bidimensional developmental model. In the minimum case, two cohorts (e.g., 1961, 1971) are observed at the same two age levels (e.g., 6, 7). A transformation of Baltes's model, with respect to the age dimension, results in the following measurements (Baltes and Nesselroade, 1969):

1. *Repeated Measurements*—leads to a series of conventional longitudinal studies for any given cohort (i.e., one sample of each cohort is observed at all age levels).
2. *Independent Measurements*—leads to a series of conventional cross-sectional studies where more than one sample is drawn from each cohort and each sample would be observed only once, at a particular age level.

From Baltes (1968, p. 159), "A repeated measurement design over the factor age is defined as one sample of the cohort y observed repeatedly, as is done in the case of the conventional longitudinal method. In contrast, independent measurements are present when several comparable samples are drawn from the cohort y which are all observed only once at a specific age level." Tables 9 and 10 depict Baltes's (1968) bidimensional developmental model for independent and repeated measures analyses respectively.

The age and cohort component analysis depicted in Table 9 fits the mathematical model $X_{ijk} = \mu + \alpha_i + \beta_j + \alpha\beta_{ij} + \xi_{ijk}$, where:

X_{ijk} = individual score
μ = population mean
α_i = treatment effect (A)
β_j = treatment effect (Co)
$\alpha\beta_{ij}$ = A x Co interaction
ξ_{ijk} = error effect

The mathematical model components depicted in Table 10 are defined as follows:

X_{ijk} = score for randomly selected entry (k) in treatment population ab_{ij} (a = level of $_i$; b = level of $_j$);
μ = grand mean of treatment levels;
α_i = treatment effect $_i$ (Co), constant for all entries within treatment population $_i$;
β_j = treatment effect $_j$ (A), constant for all entries within treatment population $_j$;
$\pi_{k(i)}$ = constant associated with entry $_k$, nested under α_i level (subjects within groups error term);
$\alpha\beta_{ij}$ = effect that represents nonadditivity of α_i and β_j effects (Co x A interaction);
$\beta\pi_{jk(i)}$ = effect that represents nonadditivity of β_j and $\pi_{k(i)}$ effects (A x subjects within groups error term);
(ijk) = experimental error term, independent of $\pi_{k(i)}$ and $\beta\pi_{jk(i)}$ error terms; in this mixed linear model, $\xi_{(ijk)}$ cannot be estimated separately from $\beta\pi_{jk(i)}$.

The analysis of variance designs illustrated in Tables 9 and 10 permits the following bidimensional developmental model delineation (Baltes, 1968, pp. 159-160):

> ... permits the separation of the main effects of age and cohort. Simultaneously, in the presence of a significant interaction between age and cohort, it is possible to infer different age effects for different levels of

TABLE 9

ANALYSIS OF VARIANCE FOR INDEPENDENT SAMPLING; AGE AND COHORT

Source of Variation	Mathematical Model Components	Degrees of Freedom
Between ages (A)	α_i	A - 1
Between cohorts (Co)	β_j	Co - 1
Age x cohort interaction	$\alpha\beta_{ij}$	(A - 1)(Co - 1)
Error	ξ_{ijk}	A Co (n - 1)
Total variation	$\mu + \alpha_i + \beta_j + \alpha\beta_{ij} + \xi_{ijk}$	n A Co - 1

TABLE 10

REPEATED MEASURES ANALYSIS OF VARIANCE; AGE AND COHORT

Source of Variation	Mathematical Model Components	Degrees of Freedom
Between subjects		n Co - 1
Between cohorts (Co)	α_i	Co - 1
Error (between subjects)	$\pi_{k(i)}$	Co (n - 1)
Within subjects		n Co (A - 1)
Between ages (A)	β_j	A - 1
Cohort x age interaction	$\alpha\beta_{ij}$	(A - 1)(Co - 1)
Error (within subjects)	$\beta\pi_{jk(i)}$	(A - 1)(n - 1) Co
Total variation	$\mu + \alpha_i + \pi_{k(i)} + \beta_j + \alpha\beta_{ij} + \beta\pi_{jk(i)} + \xi_{ijk}$	n A Co - 1

cohorts. In other words, it is possible to examine the extent to which (a) the observed behavioral characteristic is affected significantly by age, (b) the observed behavioral characteristic is affected significantly by cohort, and (c) the extent to which the effect of age is different when age is combined with specific levels of cohort. By application of suitable a posteriori tests it is subsequently possible to localize the single effects more precisely within the levels of age and cohort. Furthermore, it might be tested whether the obtained age- and cohort-functional relationships fit to some developmental trends provided by theoretical considerations or other empirical studies.

From Baltes's interpretation of the bidimensional model, it is obvious that his R = f (A, Co) model is identical to Schaie's cohort-sequential strategy. For clarification note the isomorphism of Tables 5 (Schaie's independent sampling cohort-sequential design) and 9 (Baltes's independent sampling bifactorial age x cohort design), and Tables 6 (Schaie's repeated measures cohort-sequential design) and 10 (Baltes's repeated measures bifactorial age x cohort design).

Baltes (1968) provides an informative discussion of possible outcomes of the age x cohort bidimensional design. The following examples are directly from Baltes's age x cohort design, but it is noted here that these design outcomes may be utilized for any two-factor design, e.g., Baltes's bidimensional independent sampling bifactorial model and repeated measures bifactorial model, and Schaie's cohort-sequential, cross-sequential, and time-sequential strategies. It is recommended that the reader apply Baltes's age, cohort main effects samples to Schaie's cohort-sequential (age, cohort main effects), cross-sequential (cohort, time of measurement main effects), and time-sequential (time of measurement, age main effects) strategies. In the following data outcome examples of Figure 6, Baltes utilizes a 3 (age levels, A_1, A_2, A_3) x 3 (Cohort, Co_1, Co_2, Co_3) factorial design.

Baltes (1968, pp. 161-162) discusses the above examples as follows:

> Figures [6]a[6]f represent main and interaction effects of the components age and cohort. In Figure [6]a there is neither a main nor an interaction effect since all means are on a single horizontal line. Figure [6]b shows the results of a study where a main effect of cohort only was obtained, i.e., the cohorts [$Co_1 - Co_3$] gained progressively higher scores on the dependent variable, while age had no effect. Figure [6]c represents the reverse situation. In Figure [6]d there is a main effect of age and cohort so that with increasing age as well as with increasing cohort higher scores on the dependent variable are observed. In Figure [6]e and [6]f there are interaction effects in addition to, or instead of, the main effects of age and cohort. In Figure [6]e, besides the main effects, the interaction effect is expressed by a steeper age gradient for [Co_3] than for [Co_2] and [Co_1]. Finally, Figure [6]f represents a main effect of cohort and an interaction effect since the age gradients are different for the three cohorts. There is, however, no main effect of age in Figure [6]f since the means for the three cohort groups per age level are all on a horizontal line.

Concerning the age dimension within the bidimensional model, Baltes (1968) employs the terms *cross-sectional* (CSS) and *longitudinal* (LOS) *sequences* to distinguish between a design using independent measures (CSS) and a design using repeated measurements (LOS) (see Figure 6). A *longitudinal sequence* consists of observing two or more cohorts at the same two levels (each in the sense of the conventional longitudinal method), thus confounding time of measurement. The simplest case of a longitudinal sequence is that of a 2 x 2 design with repeated measurements over the age factor. As depicted in the cells within the solid lines of Figure 7, the 5 (age) x 2 (cohort) *longitudinal sequence* is represented by cohorts 2080 and 2100 and ages 0, 20, 40, 60, and 80. The minimum 2 x 2 *longitudinal sequence* bifactorial design for Figure 7 includes cohorts 2080 and 2100 and ages 0, 20 *or* 20, 40 *or* 40, 60 *or* 60, 80. A *cross-sectional sequence* consists of observing two or more ages at the same succeeding times of measurement, thus confounding cohort. In the case of the independent observations design with regard to the age factor, it is possible to obtain the required bifactorial model observations by performing successive cross-sectional studies. As depicted in the cells within the dashed lines of Figure

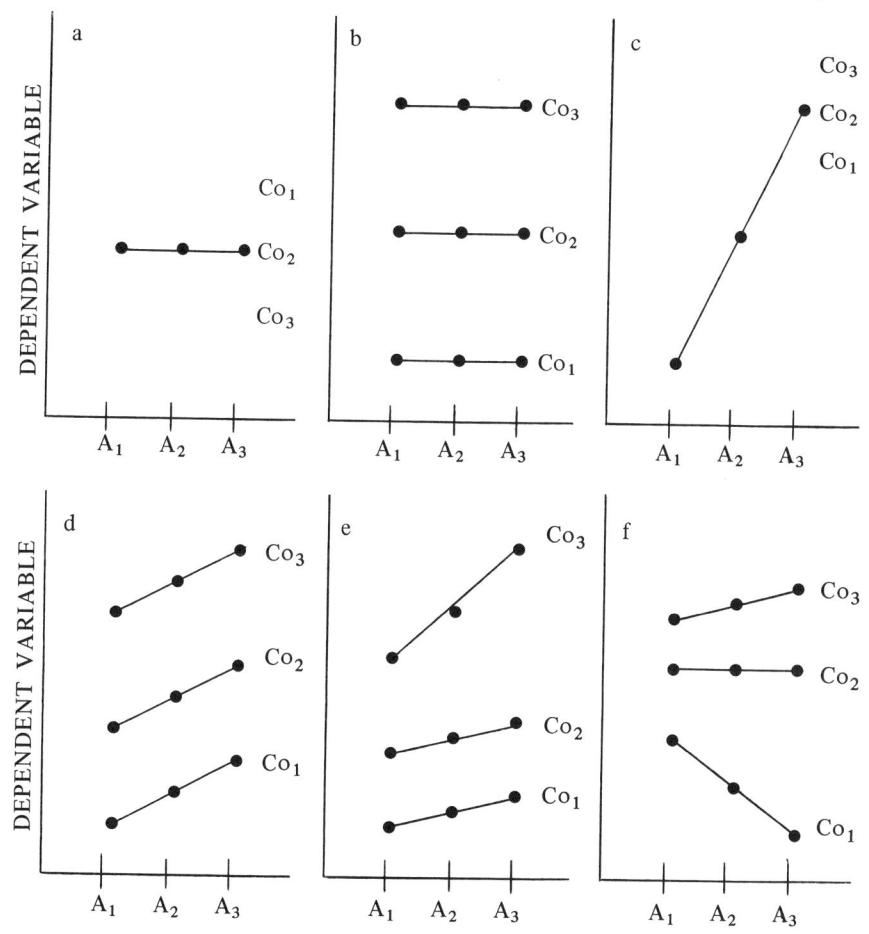

FIGURE 6 a-f. Six hypothetical outcomes of a 3 x 3 factorial design of the bifactorial developmental model; ● = means, A_1, A_2, A_3 = three levels of age, Co_1, Co_2, Co_3 = three levels of cohort (after Baltes, 1968).

7, the 5 (age) x 6 (cohort) *cross-sectional sequence* is represented by ages 0, 20, 40, 60, 80 and cohorts 2100, 2080, 2060, 2040, 2020, 2000. The minimum 2 x 2 *cross-sectional sequence* bifactorial design for Figure 7 includes ages 0 and 20 and cohorts 2100, 2080, and 2060. Finally, and as has been suggested by Baltes and Nesselroade (1969b), it is possible to simultaneously apply *cross-sectional* and *longitudinal sequences*. The argument for simultaneous implementation of sequential strategies has already been discussed in presenting Schaie's suggestion for an efficient developmental study.

A brief discussion of the practical validity of Baltes's bidimensional design is in order. Baltes's argument that the three general developmental model components—age, cohort, time of measurement—are not independent (given two, the remaining component is fixed or confounded) is appropriate. As Wohlwill (1969) and Schaie (1970) have noted, however, Baltes's bidimensional model is restrictive; that is, "the fact that the three factors age, cohort, and time of testing cannot be independently varied does not mean that it is not possible, or even desirable, to distinguish between them conceptually (just as time, distance and velocity are separate, though interdependent constructs)"

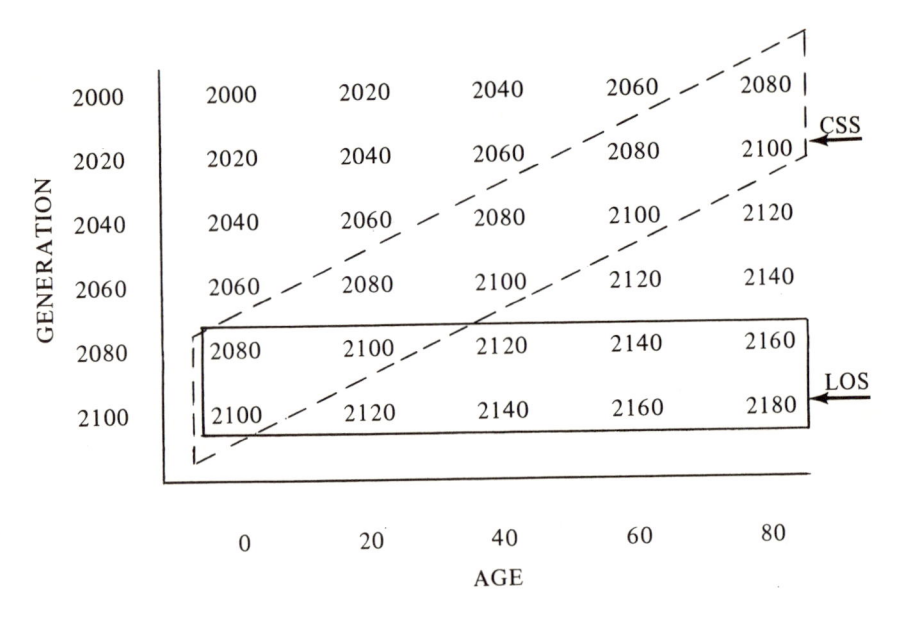

FIGURE 7. A bidimensional developmental model which can be transformed into research (data collection) strategies using either longitudinal (LOS) or cross-sectional sequences (CSS). Body entries represent corresponding time of measurement (after Baltes & Nesselroade, 1969).

(Wohlwill, 1969, p. 35). Schaie offers the following rebuttal to Baltes's bifactorial design:

> Now, it is perfectly true that the last of these three parameters can always be inferred from the other two (Baltes, 1967, 1968) but it does not follow at all that it is immaterial which two of the three parameters are independently chosen. Neither is it true that it would be possible to resolve the components of developmental change by means of a general two-factorial model. To do so, as will later be shown, one must collect data in such a way that they can be analyzed via two of the three possible two-factorial sequential strategies deducible from the three-way model. Data analysis limited to any one of the two-way models suffers from the inexorable unidirectional nature of time which must result in the spurious confounding of the third parameter which cannot be directly estimated by a single two-way design. If one begins with the three-factor model, however, one can readily derive equations which will result in independent parameter estimates by measuring over the population of ages, cohorts, or times of measurement [Schaie, 1970, p. 487].

The existence of age relationships on phenotypes is widely acknowledged (stemming from conventional cross-sectional and longitudinal findings) (Baltes and Reinert, 1969b). The sequential (series) strategies, discussed by Schaie and Baltes, emphasize the presence of cohort and environmental effects on behavior. Initial developmental studies using the sequential strategies (Baltes and Nesselroade, 1972; Baltes and Reinert, 1969; Nesselroade, 1970; Riegel, Riegel, and Meyer, 1967; Schaie, 1970; Schaie and Strother, 1968a, 1968b; Woodruff and Birren, 1972) have substantiated the need for unconfounding age, cohort, and specific environmental effects in behavioral change research.

MULTIVARIATE DATA COLLECTION DESIGNS: SEQUENTIAL STRATEGIES

Although the sequential research designs of Schaie and Baltes are more sophisticated than the conventional cross-sectional, longitudinal, and time-lag designs, the proposed sequential strategies do not always produce clear-cut and parsimonious results (see specifically Baltes and Reinert, 1969, and generally, Baltes and Nesselroade, 1969, 1970, and Schaie, 1970). Both the bidimensional and tridimensional developmental designs and resultant sequential strategies are univariate models for the analysis of long-term developmental change in a single dependent variable (R). Baltes (1968) and Schaie (1965, 1967, 1970) have thus proposed the use of univariate analysis of variance models to test for main effects and interactions, i.e., age, cohort, age x cohort or age, time of measurement, age x time of measurement. This chapter on multivariate data collection designs—dependent variables—is based primarily on the work of Baltes and Nesselroade (1969, 1970). Baltes and Nesselroade were the first to clearly suggest that the univariate developmental designs of Schaie and Baltes may be unnecessarily restrictive; i.e., such designs "may not always be sufficient in light of the multiplicity of functional relationships associated with ontogenetic and generational change" (Baltes and Nesselroade, 1969, p. 11). Thus, univariate analysis of groups with multidependent (response) measures (Baltes and Nesselroade's "multiplicity of functional relationships") rejects the theoretical or real dependence which may exist among variables. *Such rejection may ignore sources of significant differentiation between samples* (see Horton, Russell, and Moore, 1968). Baltes and Nesselroade (1972) list the following three assumptions that apply to multivariate (rather than univariate) research: "(a) *Any dependent variable (or consequent) is potentially a function of multiple determinants, (b) any determinant or antecedent has potentially multiple consequents, and (c) the study of multiple antecedent-consequent relationships provides a useful model for the organization of complex systems* such as the ontogeny of human behavior across the life-span" (p. 2). Baltes and Nesselroade have recently suggested the inclusion of multivariate *longitudinal* and *cross-sectional sequences* in the bidimensional developmental model (Baltes and Nesselroade, 1969, 1970; Nesselroade, 1970). Since Baltes's bidimensional model is basically an extension of Schaie's, it is appropriate to apply the multivariate principles to Schaie's cohort-, cross-, and time-sequential strategies. Further, it can be observed from Figure 2 that multivariate analyses fit nicely into the multiple component developmental model. That is, both the multiple component developmental model and the multivariate sequential strategies are based on the assumption of interdependency among variables.

In their initial attempts to expand the bi- and tridimensional developmental models into a more comprehensive research methodology for the analysis of long-term change, Baltes and Nesselroade draw on the concepts of Cattell's (1966) *Basic Data Relational System* and Werner (1944) and Yerkes's (1913) notion of *General Developmental Psychology*. As discussed in the previous *Developmental Design Component* chapter, Baltes expanded the original simplistic developmental paradigm of R = f (A) into a more complex developmental formulation of R = f (A, Co, T, S, Cu), where A = age, Co = cohort, T = time of measurement, S = classes of organisms in terms of species membership, and Cu = classes of organisms in terms of cultural or ecological characteristics. It was noted above that such model component expansion (multiple components) facilitates multivariate types of analysis for developmental problems. The second kind of expansion within the multidimensional model, first explicitly discussed by Baltes and Nesselroade, concerns the number of dependent behavioral variables that are simultaneously considered in a developmental investigation. The original univariate paradigm (representing the conventional, bidimensional, and tridimensional designs) was expanded into a multivariate, multidimensional paradigm:

$$R_{(1,2,\ldots,w)} = f \text{ (model components of interest)}$$

where:

$1, 2, \ldots, w$ = the number of dependent variables specified.

As noted above, within Baltes's bidimensional paradigm, data collection strategies are termed *multivariate longitudinal sequences* in the case of repeated observation (age dimension) and *multivariate cross-sectional sequences* in the case of independent observations. The essential idea of multivariate analysis is that many dependent variables are studied simultaneously. The employment of multiple dependent measures within a given program of study is certainly not new. Perhaps the best examples of research programs including analyses of multiple dependent measures are the major American longitudinal investigations—e.g., Fels Institute, University of California (Berkeley) (see Rees and Palmer, 1970). For a multiple-component developmental model, the univariate design sequences (Schaie's cohort-, time-, and cross-sequential methods; Baltes's longitudinal and cross-sectional sequences) become multivariate design sequences when R_w is greater than 1 ($R_w > 1$). As noted by Baltes and Nesselroade (1969, 1970), numerous multivariate techniques may be applied to developmental data: (a) correlational, (b) multivariate analysis of variance (MVANOV), (c) discriminant function analytical techniques, and (d) multidimensional scaling procedures. It is quickly recognized that the correlational and analysis of variance techniques are the most widely employed analytic strategies. Analysis of variance designs have usually been identified as unvariate or bivariate analyses (S-R "laws;" one or more independent variable, one dependent variable), whereas correlational designs have usually been identified as multivariate analyses (R-R "laws;" multiple dependent variables).

It would appear that a multidimensional developmental model requires multivariate analyses involving multiple independent and dependent variables. Cattell (1966) is more explicit on this point:

> . . . Certainly the rigid adherence to the classical, bivariate, analysis of variance design, because of its familiarity and simplicity, has kept many psychologists tied down to fruitless frontal attacks on problems in which at least the initial exploratory advances could have been made more rapidly by a more resourceful use of multivariate methods (p. 267).

Before discussing correlational and MVANOV techniques, it is apparent that simple matrix operations are most effective in multivariate analytic solutions.

Excellent examples of elementary matrix operations and multivariate models for evaluating phenotypic change are presented by Horst (1963b, 1966). Readers interested in basic principles of elementary matrix alegbra are referred to Horst's (1963a) readable text, *Matrix algebra for social scientists*.

Two multivariate strategies have been promoted as useful data analysis techniques for a multidimensional developmental model: MVANOV and comparative factor analysis. Baltes and Nesselroade (1969, 1970), Burt (1966), Cattell (1966), Corballis and Traub (1970), Horn (1970), Nesselroade (1970), Nunnally (1967), and Reinert (1970) have provided developmental students with excellent discussions and examples of the utility of correlational procedures in developmental construct explication. Readers interested in the basics of multivariate techniques (simultaneously dealing with a number of measurement variables)—(a) same subjects and variables (test-retest strategy), and (b) different subjects, same variables (paired-comparison strategy)—should consult Cattell (1952) or Nunnally (1967). Since multivariate comparisons (both correlational and analysis of variance) involve either test-retest or paired-comparisons strategies, it should be obvious that the univariate sequential (and classical) designs may become multivariate when $R > 1$.

It is, perhaps, necessary to caution developmental methodologists and practitioners concerning the utility of correlational procedures. It is appropriate to stress the importance of reliability and validity estimates when employing comparative factor analytic techniques. Hathaway (1965, p. 466) makes the following critical remarks in assessing the usefulness of early factor-analytically based personality inventories:[7] "Factor scales come almost magically out of the mathematical procedures that in a sense digest numerous input test variables to produce a few that account for most of the variance. Unfortunately, the new factor variables did not prove very stable with replication of the process, nor were their validities impressive." The critical point made by Hathaway and relevant to comparative factor analysis is that factor-analytically based item clusters or factor loading patterns must stand the tests of reliability and validity.

With the assumption that the reader has an elementary knowledge of correlational and factor analytic procedures (either from past experience or from taking this author's advice about Nunnally or Cattell's texts), the following discussion on comparative factor analysis consisting of comparing over levels of age and cohort covariation of specified variables is based on Baltes and Nesselroade's (1969, 1970) work. In certain instances, where it is quite necessary for the reader to understand the mechanics of factor analysis, a more detailed discussion will be provided.

---

7. Hathaway's criticism of factor-analytically based personality inventories is quite appropriate in the present context, as Baltes and Nesselroade (1969) cite studies investigating age generality of personality structure in support of comparative analysis factor loading patterns.

A PRIMER FOR DEVELOPMENTAL METHODOLOGY 81

Two types of information supplied by factor analysis and useful to developmentalists are (a) a *factor loading pattern matrix*, and (b) an *implied factor score matrix* (Baltes and Nesselroade, 1969, 1970). Both types of information are *derived* from observed data, i.e., the *data matrix*. These three matrices are defined in the following sections.

BASIC DATA MATRIX

In elementary terms, a matrix (any matrix) is a table of numbers or letters that refer to numbers with x rows and y columns. An example of a matrix is:

$$\begin{bmatrix} 3 & 8 & 1 \\ 7 & 4 & 9 \\ 3 & 2 & 6 \\ 5 & 3 & 9 \end{bmatrix}$$

The above matrix includes four rows and three columns. For the behavioral sciences, there are two types of matrices: (a) a matrix that is based on observations of people or things (e.g., measurement of dependent variables), i.e., a data matrix, and (b) a matrix that is based on a data matrix and application of certain rules, i.e., derived matrix (e.g., factor loading pattern or factor score matrix) (Horst, 1963a). A good example of the usefulness of data matrices is provided by Horst (1963a, p. 5) in the following matrix:

$$\begin{bmatrix} 2 & 1 & 2 \\ 3 & 7 & 2 \\ 0 & 1 & 4 \\ 11 & 16 & 2 \\ 0 & 0 & 2 \end{bmatrix}$$

The five rows in the above matrix may represent five different baseball teams and the columns classify runs, hits, and errors, respectively. In terms of politics, the five rows may represent five different democratic nominations for the presidency, the three columns may represent states (e.g., Michigan, Ohio, Indiana) that these candidates ran in, and the numbers may represent delegate votes committed to the respective candidates. In referring to matrices, the number of rows in a matrix is given first and the number of columns is given second. Thus, a 2 x 4 matrix refers to a matrix having two rows and four columns. The above matrix on baseball scores is a 5 x 3 data matrix. When dealing with a data matrix, rows usually represent individuals and columns usually represent scores on dependent measures or some such characteristic of the individual. Rows in general deal with *entities* (people in general, students, mental retardates) and columns in general represent *attributes* or *variables.* Thus, *entries* (e.g., numbers) within a data matrix represent how individuals scored (performed) on given variables. The following 10 x 10 data matrix (Table 11) is an example of ten individuals and their scores on the ten subtests of the Wechsler Intelligence Test for Children.[8]

Again, the rows in Table 11 represent individuals or entities, columns represent attributes or variables, and scores on the subtests (numbers in matrix) represent entries. In a general format, the basic data matrix may be represented as follows:

VARIABLES (MEASURES)

	a	b	c	d .... m
1	a_1	b_1	c_1	d_1 .... m_1
2	a_2	b_2	c_2	d_2 .... m_2
3	a_3	b_3	c_3	d_3 .... m_3
4	a_4	b_4	c_4	d_4 .... m_4
5	a_5	b_5	c_5	d_5 .... m_5
.	.	.	.	. ....
.	.	.	.	. ....
.	.	.	.	. ....
n	a_n	b_n	c_n	d_n .... m_n

PERSONS (ENTITIES)

m variables

n individuals

Horst (1963) offers several reasons for the utility of data matrices. In the behavioral (and natural sciences), the data matrix is a basis for *prediction.* In particular, prediction in the present context refers to the ability to utilize performance (scores) of specific entities (individuals) on *some* variables in attempting to predict how these individuals will perform on *other* variables. This assumption is based on the simple *Pearson r* statistic principle of establishing a measure of the relationship of variable x with variable y. Briefly, if the relationship between variables x and y is 1.00 (perfect), the researcher is able to accurately predict an individual's performance on variable y *before* he performs on measure y, given his performance on variable x. The ability to predict an

---

8. Note that the subtests are standardized, with a mean scaled score of 10 and a standard deviation of 3.

TABLE 11
10 × 10 DATA MATRIX FOR INDIVIDUAL SCORES ON WECHSLER INTELLIGENCE SCALE FOR CHILDREN

Individuals	General Information	General Comprehension	Arith.	Sim.	Voc.	Pic. Compl.	Pic. Arr.	Block Design	Object Assembly	Coding
Doug	10	12	10	10	10	10	8	14	11	12
Roger	7	7	5	8	10	12	10	13	12	10
Jean	8	8	10	10	7	13	11	15	12	13
Diane	9	9	10	10	6	10	14	12	11	14
Bill	7	6	8	10	8	10	12	13	13	11
Bob	8	9	10	11	7	12	14	11	10	12
Art	10	9	10	10	8	12	13	12	13	12
Terry	8	6	6	12	6	14	11	10	12	13
Keith	9	9	10	14	10	13	14	12	12	11
Mike	7	7	7	10	9	10	13	11	14	12

individual's performance at a later date on a *criterion* attribute (the variable the researcher wishes to predict to) from present variables (*predictor* attributes) is of extreme interest to behavioral scientists in general and testing corporations in particular. The increasing use of preschool intelligence tests (e.g., Wechsler Preschool and Primary Scale of Intelligence) is a case in point. Educators and parents are very interested in predicting a given child's academic progress even before the child enters school. Since intelligence test performance is highly related to academic performance, the use of intelligence tests to predict academic progression does seem appropriate. In our pragmatic society, it is quite the thing to be able to predict an individual's "worth" before admitting him to the program: e.g., previous academic grades, achievement tests, specific entrance tests for acceptance to undergraduate, graduate schools; ability tests, personality tests for entrance to federal, state, and private positions. To state that the American society is a test oriented one is a fair judgment. Without getting into the merits of test prediction, it is important to remember that a data matrix is a basis for predicting performance on a criterion variable given performance on a predictor variable. A first step in comparative factor analysis, then, is to establish a data matrix: rows representing entities, columns representing variables, and scores representing data entries.

DATA MATRIX AND DEVELOPMENTAL RESEARCH

Since development is included within the behavioral sciences, it is probably simplistic to state that data matrices are employed by developmentalists. For any of the classical or sequential developmental research methods, data may be included within a data matrix when $R > 1$. Assume the data matrix of Table 11 represents performance of 7-year-olds on the Wechsler subtests. If the researcher tested the same ten subjects one year later (longitudinal research design) he could construct a second data matrix (10 x 10) inclusive of the ten 8-year-olds' performance on the Wechsler subtests. Employing a cross-sectional research design, the researcher would construct two 10 x 10 matrices, one for 7-year-olds, the other for 8-year-olds. In this case, however, the researcher would have tested both age groups at approximately the same time. In terms of the sequential strategies, the researcher would construct separate matrices for each target sample; e.g., in the minimal 2 x 2 case of the time-sequential design, there are four target samples: (a) 6-years-olds, born in 1960, tested in 1966; (b) 5-year-olds, born in 1961, tested in 1966; (c) 6-year-olds, born in 1961, tested in 1967; and (d) 5-year-olds, born in 1962, tested in 1967. With the hope of not confusing the reader, the use of more than one age, cohort, or time of measurement level requires the use of several matrices (as presented above) *or* the use of a *supermatrix*. Quite simply, a supermatrix is made up of simple matrices. Thus, whereas in a simple data matrix the entries represent scores or

A PRIMER FOR DEVELOPMENTAL METHODOLOGY 85

scalars, in a supermatrix the entries represent simple matrices. Since in the above discussion of developmental related data matrices the components of age, time of measurement, or cohort include multiple levels (single component, multiple levels in classical designs, combination of any two components, multiple levels in sequential designs), the use of supermatrices as summary devices is appropriate. The usefulness of a supermatrix as a summary tool should become clear in the following example.

Assume four simple data matrices are defined as:

$$a_{11} = \begin{bmatrix} 10 & 8 & 7 & 6 \\ 12 & 10 & 8 & 10 \\ 5 & 8 & 9 & 13 \\ 10 & 14 & 9 & 8 \end{bmatrix} \quad a_{12} = \begin{bmatrix} 10 & 14 & 14 & 12 \\ 8 & 10 & 11 & 7 \\ 13 & 12 & 9 & 14 \\ 9 & 9 & 8 & 9 \end{bmatrix}$$

$$a_{21} = \begin{bmatrix} 13 & 12 & 11 & 9 \\ 10 & 7 & 10 & 9 \\ 8 & 10 & 14 & 9 \\ 11 & 12 & 9 & 9 \end{bmatrix} \quad a_{22} = \begin{bmatrix} 12 & 10 & 11 & 15 \\ 12 & 10 & 11 & 8 \\ 9 & 7 & 12 & 10 \\ 11 & 14 & 14 & 12 \end{bmatrix}$$

The above simple data matrices may be summarized in the supermatrix,

$$a = \begin{bmatrix} a_{11} & a_{12} \\ a_{21} & a_{22} \end{bmatrix}$$

Obviously the researcher may include the original simple data matrix entries within the supermatrix:

10	8	7	6	10	14	14	12
12	10	8	10	8	10	11	7
5	8	9	13	13	12	9	14
10	14	9	8	9	9	8	9
13	12	11	9	12	10	11	15
10	7	10	9	12	10	11	8
8	10	14	9	9	7	12	10
11	12	9	9	11	14	14	12

The four original simple data matrices are separated by lines and a_{11} = top left, a_{12} = top right, a_{21} = bottom left, a_{22} = bottom right.

Suppose the *entries* in each of the four simple data matrices represent individual scores on four of the Wechsler subscales. Thus for each simple data matrix, these are four individuals, each with four subscale scores. Utilizing the time-sequential design in this example,

a_{11} = 6-year-olds, born in 1960, tested in 1966 (6a of Figure 5);
a_{12} = 6-year-olds, born in 1961, tested in 1967 (6c of Figure 5);
a_{21} = 5-year-olds, born in 1961, tested in 1966 (5b of Figure 5);
a_{22} = 5-year-olds, born in 1962, tested in 1967 (5d of Figure 5).

When summarizing data for a classical or sequential design, a developmentalist may report simple matrices separately or include them within a supermatrix. Regardless of the type of data matrix utilized, developmentalists may find it quite helpful to *organize* and *manipulate* data within a data matrix. At the very least, data matrices require the researcher to separate data according to dependent variables, factors or independent variables, and levels of each independent factor.

FACTOR LOADING PATTERN MATRIX

This type of matrix is derived from, and is based on certain operations on, a data matrix. Before discussing factor loadings, it should be helpful to present the reader with an elementary presentation of factor analysis and the prerequisite correlational techniques. Factor analysis may be defined as one of several techniques for manipulating "not single variables but complexes or patterned relationships among many variables in concert" (Nesselroade, 1970, p. 195). Factor analysis is a multivariate technique for the explication or delineation of constructs; i.e., a multivariate technique for delineating " . . . the number and nature of the underlying variables [factors, abstract variables] among large number of measures [tests, dependent variables]" (Kerlinger, 1967, p. 650). Since the present Primer presents only an elementary view of factor analysis, the reader is referred to extensive discussions by Cattell (1966), Coan (1966), or Nunnally (1967). Nunnally (1967, p. 289) provides us with the following characteristics of factor analytical designs:

> Factor analysis is important mainly because it is useful in the explication of constructs [derived factor or underlying variable or hypothetical entity]. The first step in the explication of constructs is to develop measures of particular attributes which are thought to be related to the construct. . . . The second step is to correlate scores on the different measures. The correlations are analyzed to determine whether (1) all

measures are dominated by specific factors, (2) all measures are dominated by one common factor, or (3) the measures tend to break up into a number of common factors. If the analysis indicates, for example, that item 2 is the case, the third step in the explication of a construct is to perform experiments relating that construct to other constructs. "Factor analysis" is a broad term referring to numerous methods of analysis to be used in the second step described above. It is a crucial aspect of construct validation.

Basically, factor analytic techniques are derived from a correlation matrix (i.e., matrix inclusive of correlations among variables). Thus, the initial step of factor analysis proper is to compute the correlation matrix (inclusive of all study measures) which, in turn, is derived from the basic data matrix. Computational and matrix operations for deriving correlation matrices from data matrices are fully presented in readable texts by Cattell (1966) and Nunnally (1967). Briefly, these procedures deal with variance, covariance, deviation scores, and standardized score statistics to compute the degree of relationship among two or more variables. For examples of these statistics and simple correlational procedures utilizing only two variables (x and y) the reader is referred to any elementary statistical text in the behavioral sciences. Nunnally (1967) describes the computational procedures for the following most widely employed two-variable correlational statistics: *Pearson r* or *product moment* (degree of relationship between two continuous variables); *point-biserial* and *biserial* (degree of relationship between a dichotomous and continuous variable); and *rho* (degree of relationship between two sets of ranks). Utilizing the subject scores in the data matrix of Table 11, the derived correlational matrix is depicted in Table 12.

In Table 12, subtests 1 through 10 are correlated across the ten individuals; e.g., row one includes correlations r_{12} (.81), r_{13} (.70), r_{14} (.27), r_{15} (.04), r_{16} (.01), r_{17} (−.05), r_{18} (.14), r_{19} (−.33), r_{110} (.33).

Nunnally (1967) discusses several important reasons why correlational matrices are computed for factor analytic techniques:

1. The first important part played by the correlation matrix is in determining the signs and sizes of coefficients in the linear combinations that produce factors. For example, if all the correlations are positive, which tends to indicate that all the variables have something in common, it might be decided to give all variables positive weights in the first linear combination. If on the other hand, some of the variables tend to correlate negatively with the others, it might be decided to give negative weights to those. If, instead of assigning weights on some a priori basis, one derives weights mathematically in a way that optimizes some property of the data, the correlation matrix indicates how that optimization is to be done. Thus the correlation matrix is very useful in determining the signs and sizes of coefficients in linear combinations. Without the information provided by the correlation matrix, it would be very difficult to form useful linear combinations.

2. A second importance of the correlation matrix is that it greatly facilitates the correlation of variables with factors. Since each factor is a linear combination of the variables, the correlation of any variable with a factor can be obtained from the correlation of sums by the usual formulas [Nunnally, 1967, p. 196].

Cattell (1946, 1966) has defined six basic multivariate correlational techniques (on data categorized by individuals, tests or variables, and occasions of measurement) applicable to factor analytic procedures.[9] These correlational

TABLE 12

CORRELATION MATRIX FOR 10 WECHSLER SUBTESTS;
10 INDIVIDUALS OF TABLE 11

	1	2	3	4	5	6	7	8	9	10
1		.81	.70	.27	.04	.01	-.05	.14	-.33	.33
2			.72	.08	.37	-.25	-.18	.34	-.53	.16
3				.37	-.13	-.14	.31	.31	-.39	.39
4					-.07	.32	.42	-.40	-.12	.12
5						-.21	-.35	.31	.24	-.78
6							.04	-.19	-.13	.00
7								-.59	.05	.19
8									-.06	-.13
9										-.25
10										

where:
1 = General information subtest
2 = General comprehension subtest
3 = Arithmetic subtest
4 = Similarities subtest
5 = Vocabulary subtest
6 = Picture completion subtest
7 = Picture arrangement subtest
8 = Block design subtest
9 = Object assembly subtest
10 = Coding subtest

9. Coan (1966) has elaborated Cattell's three-dimensional model (six multivariate techniques) to a four-dimensional model (dependent measures, external stimuli, time of measurement, and individuals; twenty-four techniques) specifically for developmental issues.

techniques are derived from the basic data. Cattell's six basic correlational techniques are summarized as follows (Nesselroade, 1970; Nunnally, 1967):

1. *R technique:* Columns of the data matrix represent variables (tests or measures) and the rows represent individuals. This technique was employed to derive the correlational matrix of Table 12 from the data matrix of Table 11. Observing Table 11, columns represent subtests (dependent measures), rows represent individuals, and entries represent individual scores on the subtests. As noted by Nesselroade (1967), the R technique is a cross-sectional type of analysis in which measures are correlated over individuals tested at approximately the same time of measurement.

2. *P technique:* Variant of R technique; columns of the data matrix represent variables and rows represent one individual only (or average of a group of individuals) over times of measurement. Utilizing the P technique, each row represents scores on measures for the *same* individual (succeeding rows represent succeeding occasions of measurement). This technique fits within a longitudinal design, i.e., dealing with *intra-individual variation.* Since the P technique emphasizes dependent variables analysis over time, it should be clear that this design is directly applicable to age-related research.

3. *Q technique:* Utilizes the same column-row format as the R technique; columns represent variables and rows represent individuals. With the Q technique, individuals are correlated over variables ("inverse" of R technique where measures are correlated over individuals).

4. *O technique:* Variant of Q technique; utilizes the same column-row format as the P technique where rows represent the same individual over times of measurement and columns represent dependent measures. With the O technique, rows-times of measurement are correlated with one another ("inverse" of P technique where columns-variables are correlated with one another over times of measurement for one individual).

5. *S technique:* Columns represent individuals, rows represent time of measurement, and entries represent individual scores on *one* dependent measure. With the S technique, columns-individuals are correlated with one another over rows-time of measurement to derive individual dimensions or factors.

6. *T technique:* Utilizes the same column-row format as the S technique where rows represent times of measurement, columns represent individuals, and entries represent individual scores on *one* dependent measure. With the T technique, rows-times of measurement are correlated with one another over columns-individuals to derive time of measurement dimensions or factors.

Utilizing any one of the above correlational techniques, the researcher is ready to employ a specific factor analytic technique with the completion of a correlation matrix. Since factors are defined as constructs or underlying entities (deep structure) inherent in the variables, occasions, or individuals studied, factor analytic techniques refer to multivariate procedures for the explication of constructs. As will be discussed later, it is important to emphasize again that factor analysis is an integral part of construct validity. Employing the R technique as a prototype, if the correlation matrix includes only a few variables, it may be possible to "eyeball" constructs or factors. Since a factor is defined as an underlying dimension within the correlation matrix (variable covariation), if two or more variables correlate highly among themselves but not with other variables then the correlated variables share common factor variance. That is, variables that correlate highly with one another are measuring something in common. The "eyeball" technique of pulling out variable clusters or factors is illustrated in Table 13. The "eyeball" technique is a form of cluster analysis and a cluster is defined as including only those variables that correlate highly with one another (high intercorrelations) and correlate minimally with other variables (low intercorrelations) outside the cluster. Basically, a cluster in cluster analysis is the same as a factor in factor analysis.

TABLE 13

CORRELATION MATRIX AND "EYEBALLING"

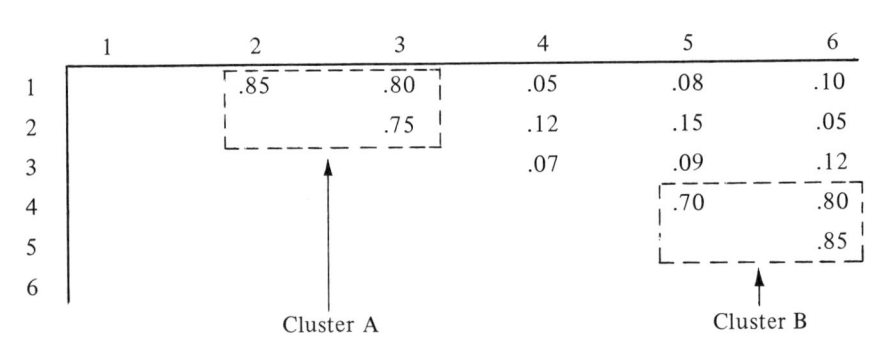

	1	2	3	4	5	6
1		.85	.80	.05	.08	.10
2			.75	.12	.15	.05
3				.07	.09	.12
4					.70	.80
5						.85
6						

Cluster A   Cluster B

where:
1 = Vocabulary subtest
2 = General comprehension subtest
3 = General information subtest
4 = Picture completion subtest
5 = Block design subtest
6 = Picture arrangement subtest

In Table 13, variables 1, 2, and 3 correlate highly with one another and correlate minimally with variables 4, 5, and 6. Variables 1, 2, and 3 represent Cluster A: these three subtests share common factor variance. Likewise, variables 4, 5, and 6 correlate highly with one another and correlate minimally with variables 1, 2, and 3. Variables 4, 5, and 6 represent Cluster B: these three subtests share common factor variance. Two factors are identified in Table 13: Clusters A and B. A problem in factor analysis and "eyeball" cluster analysis relates to defining the factors (i.e., "What do the factors mean?"). Clusters A and B (or any factors) are defined by the variables that are highly correlated within each cluster. Cluster A (subtests vocabulary, general comprehension, general information) may be defined as a verbal factor and Cluster B (subtests picture completion, block design, picture arrangement) may be defined as a performance factor.

A more sophisticated group of techniques than the correlation matrix "eyeball" method for factor explication is labeled factor analysis. The cluster analysis is improbable when many variables are involved and when clusters are not simple or clear. There are numerous techniques for the explication of factors—step-wise or indirect solutions of *centroid, principal axes,* and *square-root;* direct solutions of *group centroid, multiple group, Spearman's general-factor,* and *Holzinger's bifactor*— and the reader is referred to Harman (1967) or Nunnally (1967) for a complete discussion of factor solutions. Objective factor solutions such as the above enable the researcher to detect the number of factors derived from a correlation matrix, variable loadings on factors (correlation between variable and factor), and the magnitude of the variable-factor correlation coefficients.

A first step in any factor analytic technique is the explication of factors or underlying constructs that may exist for the variables, individuals, or occasions represented in the correlation matrix. As Horst (1966) suggests, factor extraction simplifies the information available in a correlation matrix; factor explication involves factor solution of the matrix to derive a "number of basic variables necessary to account for the observed measures within a specified degree of accuracy" (Horst, 1966, p. 146). The smaller number of variables (basic variables) are termed factors. After factors have been explicated from the correlation matrix by a factor solution (i.e., intercorrelation of variables), a second aspect of factor analysis is to compute the *factor loadings*. As mentioned above, a factor loading simply refers to the correlation (or relationship) between a variable and a factor. A factor loading pattern matrix consists of correlations among variables (of data, covariance, and correlation matrices) and factors. For a factor loading pattern matrix, there are as many columns as extracted factors and as many rows as variables or measures. For a set of n variables, the linear model ($z_j = a_{j_1} F_1 + a_{j_2} F_2 + \ldots + a_{jm} F_m + d_j u_j$; $j = 1, 2, \ldots, n$) expressing any variable z_j in terms of m common factors and its unique factor may be written in the following expanded form. This set of equations is termed a factor pattern and the coefficients of the factors are referred to as loadings (i.e., correlations of variables with factor scores) (Harmon, 1967):

$$z_1 = a_{11}F_1 + a_{12}F_2 + \ldots + a_{1m}F_m + d_1U_1$$
$$z_2 = a_{21}F_1 + a_{22}F_2 + \ldots + a_{2n}F_m \quad\quad + d_2U_2$$
$$\cdot \quad\quad \cdot \quad\quad \cdot \quad\quad \ldots \quad\quad \cdot$$
$$z_n = a_{n1}F_1 + a_{n2}F_2 + \ldots + a_{nm}F_m \quad\quad + d_nU_n$$

The following factor loading matrix is based on hypothetical data:

		Factors			h^2
		A	B	C	
Variables	1	.80	.00	.25	.70
	2	.71	.02	.03	.51
	3	.82	.00	.01	.67
	4	.01	.72	.10	.53
	5	.10	.75	.12	.59
Sum of Squared loadings		1.83	1.08	.09	
S^2 Factor		.37	.22	.02	.61

The entries in this 5 x 3 factor loading matrix represent variable-factor correlations. Two factors (A, B) account for most of the inter-variable relationships: factor A includes variables 1, 2, and 3 with high loadings and variables 4 and 5 with low loadings; factor B includes variables 4 and 5 with high loadings and variables 1, 2, and 3 with low loadings. All five variables load minimally on factor C. *Squaring a variable-factor coefficient represents the proportion of variance explained by a factor for a variable;* e.g., $(.80)^2 = .64 =$ proportion of variance accounted for by factor A for variable 1. *The sum of squared loadings for each column represents the total amount of variance accounted for by a factor for all five variables;* e.g., sum of squared variable loadings for factor A equals 1.83. *The S^2 factor row represents the average squared loadings for each factor, i.e.,* S^2 factor for each column equals the proportion of variance accounted for by a factor for all five variables as a group. For example, factor A accounts for 37 percent of the total variance in the original data matrix. *The sum of the S^2 factors (.61) represents the proportion of variance accounted for by all three factors.* Thus, factors A, B, and C account for 61 percent of the total variance in the original data matrix; 61 percent of the total variance (1.0) in the original data matrix or derived correlation matrix is explained by the three factors. Finally, *h^2 refers to the sum of squared loadings in any row and* *represents the proportion of variance of any variable which is accounted for by the three factors.* For example, 70 percent of the variance of variable 1 is accounted for by factors A, B, and C. Since only variables 1, 2, and 3 load highly on factor A, these variables define the factor. Likewise, only variables 4 and 5 load highly on factor B and define it. To summarize this brief introduction to factor loadings, it is again emphasized that a factor loading pattern matrix provides the following information: (a) number of factors extracted (reduced number of variables needed to define total number of variables manipulated in a given study; (b) variable-factor loadings (proportion of variable variance attributable to a given factor); (c) total proportion of a given variable variance accounted for by all extracted factors; (d) total variable variance accounted for by a given factor; and (e) total variable — data matrix — variance accounted for by all factors. In general, the factor loading pattern matrix is most often utilized to describe the structure or organization among the variables studied; e.g., all study variables measure the same thing (high variable intercorrelations, one factor accounts for most of the common variance), or study variables measure different things (high, middle, low variable intercorrelations, more than one factor needed to account for total variable variance). Thus, once factors have been explicated, defining such factors stems from interpretations of what the variables are that load high on factors.

An example of employing a factor loading pattern matrix for organizing the variables under study deals with Nihira's (1969) study on factorial dimensions of adaptive behavior of mentally retarded individuals. Nihira researched the primary dimensions on which adult institutionalized retardates differ among themselves in adapting with the environment. The following twenty-five variables were included within the multivariate study:

1. Independent Functioning
2. Physical Development
3. Economic Activities
4. Language Development
5. Number and Time Concept
6. Occupation (Domestic)
7. Occupation (General)
8. Self-Direction
9. Responsibility
10. Socialization
11. Violent and Destructive Behavior
12. Anti-Social Behavior
13. Rebellious Behavior
14. Untrustworthy Behavior
15. Socially Unacceptable Manners
16. Withdrawal
17. Stereotyped Behavior
18. Self-Abusive Behavior
19. Peculiar and Eccentric Habits
20. Sexually Aberrant Behavior
21. Psychological Disturbances
22. Use of Medication
23. Age
24. Institution
25. Sex

Variables 1 through 22 are based on rating scales (retardate rated on each of the twenty-two variables by a psychiatric aide). Variables 23 (age), 24 (institution), and 25 (sex) are organismic-demographic variables. Table 14 depicts the factor loading pattern matrix with twenty-five variables and the resulting variable-factor coefficients for six factors.

TABLE 14

ROTATED FACTOR MATRIX[a]

Variable Number	I	II	III	IV	V	VI	h^2
1	84[b]	12	16	-18	34	-12	90
2	51	12	17	-09	31	-05	41
3	75	10	22	-11	16	-06	66
4	79	21	30	-24	-02	00	82
5	73	05	35	-22	06	05	71
6	62	14	39	02	-03	-18	59
7	84	01	06	-03	11	-20	77
8	82	-17	-14	-06	08	03	73
9	80	-05	02	-08	00	-22	70
10	78	-22	-06	-13	-00	05	68
11	-19	57	-07	24	-15	19	49
12	21	68	-03	13	-14	10	56
13	-11	71	10	-00	09	10	54
14	14	67	-01	00	-06	-00	47
15	-31	40	01	34	-06	10	39
16	-51	-10	18	20	18	-11	39
17	-44	15	15	34	05	15	37
18	-37	24	-11	30	-07	25	36
19	-34	24	-09	28	-03	-11	27
20	-16	20	-05	17	-04	27	17
21	10	66	07	05	-01	07	46
22	-12	12	11	21	-02	08	10
23	01	-09	-03	-02	-01	-39	17
24	13	-01	53	05	05	03	30
25	-09	13	-03	01	-47	-01	24
Factor Variance	6.70	2.74	.88	.78	.59	.56	
Percentage of Variance[c]	54.6%	22.4%	7.2%	6.4%	4.8%	4.6%	

[a]The six principal axes were rotated orthogonally to the varimax interim. Factor rotation was done to obtain a more interpretable pattern of factor loadings.
[b]Decimal point omitted.
[c]Sums of squares of factor loadings.

Following Nihira, the factors were interpreted as follows:

FACTOR I: *Personal Independence*

Variables	Factor Loadings
7 Occupation (General)	.84
1 Independent Functioning	.84 (.34 V)[a]
8 Self-Direction	.82
9 Responsibility	.80
4 Language Development	.79 (.30 III)
10 Socialization	.78
3 Economic Activities	.75
5 Number and Time Concepts	.73 (.35 III)
6 Occupation (Domestic)	.62 (.39 III)
2 Physical Development	.51 (.31 V)
15 Socially Unacceptable Manners	−.31 (.40 II; .34 IV)
19 Peculiar and Eccentric Habits	−.34 (.28 IV)
18 Self-Abusive Behavior	−.37 (.30 IV; .25 VI)
17 Stereotyped Behavior	−.44 (.34 IV)
16 Withdrawal	−.51

[a]Variable loading on second factor.

All variables with significantly high positive loadings on this factor, except Self-Direction and Responsibility, represent important skills and abilities required to maintain personal independence.
. . . The factor clearly involves both skills and abilities as well as the presence or lack of motivational force toward the maintenance of personal independence. Therefore, it is tentatively labeled "Personal Independence" [pp. 873-874].

FACTOR II: *Social Maladaptation*

Variables	Factor Loadings
13 Rebellious Behavior	.71
12 Anti-Social Behavior	.68
14 Untrustworthy Behavior	.67
21 Psychological Disturbances	.66
11 Violent and Destructive Behavior	.57
15 Socially Unacceptable Manners	.40 (.34 I)

This factor refers to a broad, general dimension of social maladaptation which includes destructiveness, rebelliousness, untrustworthiness, antisocial behaviors and manners, and personality problems indicating various negative attitudes toward the social environment.
. . . Because of its anti-social, extrapunitive elements, the present factor is tentatively labeled "Social Maladaptation" [pp. 874-875].

FACTOR III: *Institutional Difference*

Variables	Factor Loadings
24 Institution	.53
6 Occupation (Domestic)	.39 (.62 I)
5 Number and Time Concepts	.35 (.73 I)
4 Language Development	.30 (.79 I)

Since this factor is primarily defined by Variable 24, Institution, alone, it is best interpreted as the factor of institutional difference [p. 875].

FACTOR IV: *Intra-Maladaptation*

Variables	Factor Loadings
17 Stereotyped Behavior	.34 (−.44 I)
15 Socially Unacceptable Manners	.34 (.40 II; −.31 I)
18 Self-Abusive Behavior	.30 (−.37 I; .25 VI)
19 Peculiar and Eccentric Habits	.28 (−.34 I)

The variables defining this factor suggest a self-depreciative, self-castigating, and intrapunitive type of disorganization in the adaptive process as opposed to the extrapunitive, anti-social maladaptation as in the case of Factor II. For this reason, this factor may be called either "Intra-Maladaptation" or "Personal Maladaptation."
 ... the fact that all variables defining this factor also appear strongly on Factor I raises a question about the significance of this factor and prevents clear interpretation of its meaning [p. 875].

FACTOR V: *Sex Difference*

Variables	Factor Loadings
1 Independent Functioning	.34 (.84 I)
2 Physical Development	.31 (.51 I)
25 Sex: Male = 1, Female = 2	−.47

Since this factor is primarily defined by Variable 25, Sex, alone, it is best interpreted as the factor of sex difference. Independent Functioning and Physical Development have secondary but significant loadings on this factor. This indicates that the female subjects were rated lower as a group than male subjects with respect to these variables [p. 875].

FACTOR VI: *Age Difference*

Variables	Factor Loadings
20 Sexually Aberrant Behavior	.27
18 Self-Abusive Behavior	.25 (−.37 I; .30 IV)
23 Age	−.39

This factor is primarily defined by Variable 23, Age, and Variable 20, Sexually Aberrant Behavior. The negative loading of the age variable indicates that Sexually Aberrant Behavior is inversely related to age, i.e., such behaviors are more frequently observed among younger residents than among older residents [p. 876].

Perhaps the most pedagogical aspect of the above example is that the factor analysis performed by Nihira reduced the twenty-five variables to six underlying factors. These six factors accounted for approximately 95 percent of the original data matrix. A second aspect of the example is the clear use of high loading variables to define a given factor.

FACTOR LOADING PATTERN MATRIX AND DEVELOPMENTAL RESEARCH

As noted by Baltes and Nesselroade (1969, 1970), *comparison* of factor loading patterns or clusters was initially utilized in interpretive research on intellectual structure, an area of development. These methodologists also pointed out, quite appropriately, that the early intelligence data factor loading comparisons (e.g., over age groups) did not deal with the criticism of developmental model component confounding. That is, such factor loading comparative studies were either cross-sectional (age main effect, cohort component confounded) or longitudinal (age main effect, time of measurement component confounded).[10] It is presently argued that contemporary comparative factor loading studies of intellectual abilities, which still utilize the classical developmental designs, are subject to the same criticism of developmental model component confounding.

---

10. The use of classical developmental designs for age related comparative investigations on factor loading patterns of intellectual abilities resulted in conflicting findings and controversy (see Baltes and Nesselroade, 1969). This problematic result of utilizing classical designs in multivariate research is similar to that reported by Schaie (page 32 of text) for univariate research.

In discussing the usefulness of developmental-comparative factor loading pattern research, Baltes and Nesselroade note the importance of invariance of factor loading patterns:

> ... The highest type of factor invariance to be achieved in comparing the factor loading patterns of different samples of age and generation, measured on the same variables, would be that the factor loading patterns are identical or, at least proportional. Perfect invariance would imply that a common structure underlies the variance-covariance matrices estimated from observed scores on the variables of the different samples of age and generation. Thus, in case of perfect invariance, we would infer that the constructs or concepts (factors determined by factor analysis) relate to observables (tests) in precisely the same way for the different comparison groups, and that the internal structure (Nunnally, 1967) of constructs could be regarded as being qualitatively the same [1970, p. 164].

The notion of factor loading pattern invariance applies to all multivariate applications of developmental sequential strategies, not just Baltes's multivariate longitudinal and cross-sectional sequences. For any of Schaie's sequential strategies (dependent and independent sampling) it is possible to assess factor loading pattern invariance for the two independently manipulated developmental model components and the interaction effect. For example, with the time-sequential design the researcher would be able to assess comparative factor loading invariance over the age and time of measurement levels and the samples within the age x time of measurement interaction. For the sequential strategies employing repeated measures (cohort- and cross-sequential), the assessment of factor loading invariance between independent samples and corresponding dependent samples would provide evidence of practice effects.

FACTOR SCORES

Whereas factor loading patterns depict the multiple relationships between variables (test, subtests) and factors (constructs), factor scores represent (in elementary terms) the scores of individuals on a factor. Detailed discussions of techniques for estimating factor scores (exact scores, regression estimates, composite estimates, basic variable) are available in Harman (1967, 1968), Horn (1965) and Rummel (1970). Rummel (p. 435) provides the following example depicting the relationships among raw data, factor loadings, and factor scores.

Let there be three cases, a, b, and c, with data x_{aj}, x_{bj}, and x_{cj} on variable X_j. Let the factor loadings of X_j on two factors, S_1 and S_2, be α_{j1} and α_{j2}. Also let the factor scores for the three cases on S_1 be s_{a1}, s_{b1}, and s_{c1}, and on S_2 let them be s_{a2}, s_{b2}, and s_{c2}. Then the factor model for component analysis is:

A PRIMER FOR DEVELOPMENTAL METHODOLOGY

$$\begin{bmatrix} X_{aj} \\ X_{bj} \\ X_{cj} \end{bmatrix} = \alpha_{j1} \begin{bmatrix} S_{a1} \\ S_{b1} \\ S_{c1} \end{bmatrix} + \alpha_{j2} \begin{bmatrix} S_{a2} \\ S_{b2} \\ S_{c2} \end{bmatrix}$$

$$X_j \qquad\qquad S_1 \qquad\qquad S_2$$

Nesselroade (1970) also depicts the relationship of individual raw scores, factor loadings, and factor scores in the following equation:

$$a_{ji} = b_{j1} F_{1i} + b_{j2} F_{2i} + \ldots + b_{jk} F_{ki} + S_{ji}$$

where:

a_{ji} = measured response of individual i;

b_j = weights or factor loadings, representing factor contributions to performance a_j ($b_{j1}, b_{j2}, \ldots, b_{jk}$);

F_i = individual i's factor scores;

S_{ji} = unique model component specific to individual i's measured response, a_j.

Following Nesselroade, b_j model components are not referenced to specific individuals. That is, b_j components represent relationships among variables and factors (factor loadings). The F_i model components (factor scores) represent an individual's scores on particular factors, not particular variables. In a second equation, Nesselroade depicts the importance of differentiating factor score from factor loading analyses in comparative (e.g., age-related) research.

$$a_{ji}' = b_{j1} F_{1i}' + b_{j2} F_{2i}' + \ldots + b_{jk} F_{ki}' + S_{ji}'$$

where:

a_{ji}' = represents measured response of individual at a succeeding time of measurement.

Observing the above two equations, it can be seen that the factor loadings (b_j, b_j) are the same, but factor scores are different (F_i, F_i'). It is, of course, possible that the researcher may find factor loading differences with successive times of measurement (b_j, b_j').

FACTOR SCORES AND DEVELOPMENTAL RESEARCH

Baltes and Nesselroade (1970, 1972; Nesselroade, 1970) suggest that comparatively invariant (matched) to variant (unmatched) *factor loading patterns* represent qualitative comparisons and the *factor score* comparisons represent quantitative change. Thus, a comparative analysis of factor loading invariance permits assessment of possible change in factor-variable relationships (any significant change referred to as a qualitative one). On the other hand, comparative analysis (inter- or intra-individual variation) of factor scores (individual or mean-factor relationship) permits assessment of possible change in levels within a dimension or factor (any significant change referred to as a quantitative one). A simple illustrative case based on the variant-invariant factor loading and stable-fluctuant factor score components is as follows: A factor loading pattern may or may not remain (completely identical or completely proportional) invariant over the life span—psychological trait (dependency) or maturational principle (physical-psychological construct of proximodistal growth gradient)—and tested individuals may or may not maintain their relative levels or positions on invariant factors. Baltes and Nesselroade (1972; Nesselroade, 1967) have delineated the 2 factor loading (variant, invariant) x 2 factor score (stable, fluctuant) classification scheme as follows:

a. *Invariant loading patterns—stable factor scores*
b. *Invariant loading patterns—fluctuant factor scores*
c. *Noninvariant loading patterns—stable factor scores*
d. *Noninvariant loading patterns—fluctuant factor scores*

1. Type-a factors (Invariant Patterns—Stable Scores) have the characteristics of ideal traits, in the conventional sense. The invariant patterns denote a high degree of repeatability, at least over relatively short time spans, of the interrelationships of responses. The stable factor scores indicate that subjects are maintaining their relative positions on the dimensions inferred from these highly repeatable response patterns.

2. Type-b factors (Invariant Patterns—Fluctuant Scores), also evince repeatable response patterns, but the fluctuant rather than stable factor scores indicate that persons do not maintain their relative positions, over time, on the factor score continua. Factors of this type best fit the traditional notion of state dimensions. To illustrate this more clearly we might be able to identify, with appropriate measures, a highly consistent and well-known behavior pattern for which a college student scoring high on the dimension on Saturday night would place lower on the scale on Sunday morning than his less enterprising peers . . . .

3. Type-c factors (Noninvariant Patterns—Stable Scores) appear to have a substantive parallel in, for example, behavior patterns displayed during transition, critical, or crisis periods, etc. Suppose subjects in a sample are distributed such that on a set of conservation tasks some consistently manage to conserve on only three, some on five, or six, and some nine or ten tasks. Regardless of the number of tasks on which they conserve, however, they succeed on different patterns of tasks at different times. Data such as these could show Type-c factors if the loading patterns would differ from one testing period to the next while the ordering of subjects along a continuum representing conservation behavior remained stable . . . .

4. Type-d factors might be summarily dismissed, in a short term context, as either error factors, situation specific factors, or some other

type of non-repeatable "transients." In a life-span perspective, however, Type-d factors may be useful. One might assume, for example, that in early phases of ontogeny responses are somewhat unstable and independent of each other, similar to a situation of relative chaos. Subsequent ontogeny would then consist of an imposition of order on the initial state of specificity [Baltes and Nesselroade, 1972, pp. 8-10].

In concluding this section on factor analytic components within a developmental framework, it is emphasized that any developmental design (classical, sequential) may incorporate analyses of factor loadings and factor scores for assessment of *inter*-individual variability. Based on the earlier discussion of the benefits of the longitudinal design (page 30), it should be clear that only repeated measures developmental designs (longitudinal, repeated measures sequential) may incorporate analyses of factor loadings and factor scores for assessment of *intra*-individual variability.

MULTIVARIATE ANALYSIS OF VARIANCE (MVANOV)

Although the use of comparative factor analytic techniques is relatively high, there has been little integration of the utility of MVANOV designs in developmental construct explication. As Jones (1966, p. 245) states:

[MVANOV], like the more familiar univariate analysis of variance, focuses upon differences between groups or between experimental conditions. In this sense, it may be contrasted with correlational methods, which apply to within-group inter-individual relations. In analysis of variance the matter at issue is that of systematic differences in performance between groups of subjects, with groups defined by the levels of classification of one or more independent variables.

Cattell (1966) has noted that in regard to the independent variable, classical univariate analysis of variance designs are semi-multivariate (*unilaterally multivariate*); i.e., multiple levels and/or independent variables. When analyzing more than one dependent variable, the analytic method of choice is *bilaterally multivariate*. If more than one dependent variable is included within a research paradigm, the difference between employing a unilateral versus a bilateral multivariate method is that "the relative importance of each variable may be quite different when all are considered jointly [MVANOV] than when each is considered marginally [analysis of variance]" (Aitkin, 1971, p. 236). Aitkin goes on to state:

This phenomenon is quite familiar in multiple regression (which is often considered not to be a multivariate technique), where some predictor variables which are uncorrelated with the criterion may appear with large regression coefficients, while some with high correlations may appear with zero regression coefficients (p. 236).

Numerous discussions (including research examples) of MVANOV methods are available: Aitkin (1971), Anderson (1958), Bock (1963), Bock and Haggard (1968), Burt (1966), Cole and Grizzle (1966), Cooley and Lohnes (1962, 1971), Horton, Russell, and Moore (1968), Jones (1966), Morrison (1967), and Tatsuoka (1971). Usually, multivariate developmental research involves multivariate independent and dependent variables. Bock and Haggard offer the following summary statement regarding MVANOV: "The purpose in applying multivariate statistical analysis to [multivariate problems] is to determine how and to what extent the independent variables explain or predict the responses of the subjects represented in the dependent variables" (1968, p. 100).

A simple example of a bifactorial MVANOV provided by Tatsuoka (1971) should introduce the reader to elementary MVANOV. Since this example utilizes data and derived matrices, the reader may find it beneficial to look again at pages 81-98. Following Jones (1966), the principle components of a MVANOV design are as follows:

Given:

t = dimensions of MVANOV design (t_1 = 1 dimensional, t_2 = 2 dimensional, etc.);

q = dependent variables, i.e., scores obtained for each subject (q_1 = 1 dependent variable, q_2 = 2 dependent variables, etc.);

a = levels of independent variables or number of independent variables within one dimension (a_1 = 1 level within first dimension, a_2 = 2 levels within first dimension, etc.);

b = levels of independent variables or number of independent variables within a second dimension (b_1 = 1 level within second dimension, b_2 = 2 levels within second dimension, etc.);

c = levels of independent variables or number of independent variables within a third dimension (c_1 = 1 level within third dimension, c_2 = 2 levels within third dimension, etc.);

It follows that:

The design is a q variate, t classification design.

Some derivations: where

$a = 1, q = 1$: univariate analysis of variance design,
$a > 1, q = 1$: semi-multivariate or unilaterally MVANOV design,
$a > 1, q > 1$: bilaterally MVANOV design,
$t > 1, q > 1$: bilaterally MVANOV design.

Table 15 depicts Jones's (1966) 2-way MVANOV ($t = 2, q > 1$). The entries in the $t = 2$ x $q > 1$ MVANOV design illustrated in Table 15 represent mean

TABLE 15
MEAN VECTORS FOR A $t = 2 \times q$ 1 MVANOV

	1	2	...	j	...	b	Row Mean
1	X_{11}	X_{12}	...	X_{1j}	...	X_{1b}	$X_{1..}$
2	X_{21}	S_{22}	...	X_{2j}	...	X_{2b}	$S_{2..}$
.	.	.	...	.	...	.	.
i	X_{i1}	X_{i2}	...	X_{ij}	...	X_{ib}	X_i
.	.	.	...	.	...	.	.
a	X_{a1}	X_{a2}	...	X_{aj}	...	X_{ab}	$X_{a..}$
Column Mean	$X_{.1.}$	$X_{.2.}$	...	$X_{.j.}$	...	$X_{.b.}$	$X_{..}$

vectors,[11] i.e., the mean of subject (m_{ij}) observation vectors. Thus, the cell entries in the table represent mean dependent scores for each subject on two dimensions (a = dimension 1, b = dimension 2).

Since the computational and/or matrix procedures are beyond the scope of this Primer, the interested reader is referred to Tatsuoka (1971, Chapter 7) for a rather complete introduction to such material. Perhaps the most important advantage of applying MVANOV designs to developmental issues is that of assessing the separate and combined effects of independent and/or organismic variables on one or multiple dependent variables. Such variable relationships as the following, although usually studied within a univariate design, would be quite feasible within a multivariate design.

Independent variable	*Organismic variable*	*Dependent variable*
A. Socioeconomic status	a. Age	1. Intelligence
B. Culture	b. Sex	2. Anxiety
C. Subculture	c. Race	3. Height
D. Prenatal environment	d. Physical impairments	4. Conservation

11. A vector is a matrix with only one row *or* one column; an example of a row vector is [3,8,12]; an example of a column vector is $\begin{bmatrix} 3 \\ 8 \\ 12 \end{bmatrix}$. Each entry in Table 15 represents a $q \times 1$ column vector, the mean of m_{ij} raw data (observation) vectors, for each subject

Independent variable	Organismic variable (cont.)	Dependent variable
E. Preschool environment	e. Genetic manipulation	5. Problem-solving
F. Child-rearing practice		6. Attitudes
G. Institutionalization		7. Concept attainment
H. Reinforcement paradigms		8. Cognitive styles
I. Learning models		9. Memory
J. Situational factors		10. Perception
K. Drugs		11. Language

Almost all developmental and behavioral analysis of variance design research is what Cattell has termed semi-multivariate or unilaterally multivariate, i.e., several independent variables manipulated and effects assessed on one dependent variable. Employing the above paradigm, a typical case of developmental research involves variables A, a, 1. That is, a number of socioeconomic status groups (A_1, A_2) and a number of ages (a_1, a_2) are included within a univariate or unilaterally multivariate design with IQ score as the dependent variable. Fairly recently, the "intelligence" variable has been delineated into (a) full scale IQ score, verbal IQ score, and performance IQ score, or (b) all subtests of an IQ test (e.g., Wechsler 10 subtests). Even if more than one dependent variable is included within a developmental design (*a* and *b* above), the effects of independent-organismic variables are assessed on each dependent variable separately. The simple fact is that even when more than one dependent variable is included within a research project, it is seldom that researchers assess the interrelationships of such variables in an analysis of variance design. It is important to remember that complex analysis of variance designs are multivariate in nature (e.g., factorial designs), with more than one independent variable. These complex designs are termed unilaterally multivariate; i.e., multivariate in the sense of multiple independent variables. Bilaterally multivariate designs include multiple independent *and* dependent variables. Since MVANOV designs reflect the various requirements of univariate analysis of variance designs—particularly those of independent sampling and repeated measures—it is evident that the multiple variable designs are applicable to classic and sequential developmental strategies. And, as the multiple component developmental model emphasizes numerous factors associated with given phenotype developments, it follows that MVANOV (as well as correlational) designs should be utilized to analyze for possible multiple variate interdependency. Simply stated, it is reasonable to assume that some or all (more than one) of the developmental model components must be considered together on one or more dependent variables.

CONSTRUCT DELINEATION

A final point should be made concerning the multidimensional developmental model and multivariate research strategies. Multivariate research problems within the general developmental model usually center on abstract concepts or constructs, i.e., intelligence, personality. That is, when employing multivariate strategies, the researcher is typically dealing with multiple referents of one or more constructs. In fact, as noted by Nesselroade (1970, pp. 195-196):

> Without involving ourselves in fruitless debate over such issues as the status of derived variables, such as factors, as psychological constructs, let us admit that there are advantages to being able to examine and, possibly, even to manipulate not single variables but complexes or patterned relationships among many variables in concert. This necessarily involves some degree of abstraction, although one may choose not to move too far from hard data.
>
> It is basic to the "multivariate ethic," however, that the abstractions, concepts, or constructs, with which segments of behavioral science must ultimately deal, are not adequately indexed by single, observable responses (Cattell, 1946, 1968; Cronbach, 1957). To the extent that one is willing to operate in terms of abstractions or concepts derived from data there are two related and well-recognized aspects involved in making such identifications; both of which can be efficiently treated within a multivariate framework. The first is that of finding out what measures "belong" to the concept; the second is that of determining what measures do not "belong."

Nunnally offers an excellent discussion of the problem of construct explication within multidimensional, multivariate models:

> Strictly speaking, scientists can never be sure that a construct has been measured or that a theory regarding that construct has been tested, even though it may be useful to speak as though such were the case. A construct is only a word, and although the word may suggest explorations of the internal structure of an interesting set of variables, there is no way to prove that any combination of those variables actually "measures" the word. . . . Call it the "measurement" and "validity" of constructs if you like, but at least as far as science takes us, there are only (1) words denoting constructs, (2) sets of variables specified for such constructs, (3) evidence concerning internal structures of such sets, (4) words concerning relations among constructs (theories), (5) which suggest cross-structure among sets of observables, (6) evidence regarding such cross-structures, and (7) beyond that, nothing (1967, pp. 98-99).

Nunnally's comments on construct explication are important for theorists and researchers in any discipline to ponder. His points are stressed in this Primer because of the two advancements in development introduced in Chapter 1; i.e., a multiple component developmental model and univariate and multivariate design advances to classical developmental strategies. Many variables (independent, organismic, dependent) manipulated in developmental investigations, particularly those in psychological and sociological development, are abstract rather than concrete. It should also be emphasized that many developmental univariate investigations, as well as multivariate research, deal with constructs that are loosely defined. That is, many abstract variables—constructs—of interest to developmentalists (e.g., intelligence, personality, anxiety, behavioral proximodistal growth gradient) have numerous referents (behavioral observations) that may or may not be significantly intercorrelated. In fact, the historical controversy in development reflects the lack of construct explication of two abstract variables—heredity (genetics) and environment (physical, psychological, social). These constructs (really belief systems) are large (abundance of referents or defining variables) and loosely defined. The point made here is that it is one thing to employ (a) a single (age) vs. multiple component developmental model (see Figure 2), (b) univariate vs. multivariate classical design, and (c) univariate vs. multivariate sequential design, but quite another to attempt to explain inter- or intra-individual differences on constructs. Nunnally (1967) has presented three stages of construct delineation as follows:

1. Specifying the domain of observables for a given construct. What variables adequately define intelligence?
2. Determining to what extent all, or some, of the specified observables in *1* correlate with each other and/or are similarly affected by experimental treatments (independent variables).
3. Assessing whether or not measures of variables in *2 act* as though they measure the construct in *1*.

> Aspect 3 consists of determining whether or not a supposed measure of a construct correlates in expected ways with measures of other constructs or is affected in expected ways by particular experimental treatments. These steps are seldom, if ever, purposefully planned and undertaken by any investigator or group of investigators. Also, although it could be argued that the aspects should be undertaken in the order 1, 2, and then 3, this order is seldom, if ever, followed. More likely, a psychologist will develop a particular measure that is thought to partake of a construct, then he will leap directly to aspect 3 and perform a study relating the supposed measure of the construct to measures of other constructs, e.g., correlating a particular measure of anxiety with a particular measure of response to frustration. Typically, other investigators will develop other particular measures of the same construct, and skipping aspects 1 and 2, they will move directly to aspect 3 and try to find interesting relations between their measures and measures of other constructs. As the number of proposed measures of the same construct grows and suspicion grows that they might not all measure the same thing, one or more investigators seek to outline in writing the domain of observables related to the construct, which is aspect 1. All, or parts, of one or more such outlines of the domain

are subjected to investigation to determine the extent to which variables in the domain tend to measure the same thing, which is aspect 2. The impact of theorizing with respect to aspect 1 and the research results from aspect 2 tend to influence which particular variables are studied in aspect 3 [p. 87].

A logical extension of Nunnally's argument is that his step *1* (specification of construct referents) corresponds to delineation of factors or components in a multiple component developmental model. Nunnally's comment on construct explication in general is quite appropriate in the area of development: "Instead of the domain observables for any construct being tightly defined initially (step 1), more likely the nature of the domain will be *suggested* by numerous attempts to develop particular measures relating to the construct; and subsequently some investigators will attempt to more explicity outline the domain of content" (p. 88). To obtain maximum effect of empirical investigations on constructs or model components (steps *2* and *3*) with adequate developmental designs (univariate and multivariate), developmentalists need to recognize a *grand plan* (multiple component developmental model). As students and instructors well know, there are a multitude of facts, principles, and theories in the area of development. Unfortunately, most facts are independent, most principles rely on loosely defined, broad constructs, and most theories (based on selected facts and principles) are too restrictive.

CONCLUDING COMMENTS

IT IS HOPED THAT the material presented in this Primer has not discouraged those students of behavioral change who appreciate the need for (a) life-span guidelines, (b) a multiple component developmental model, and (c) sophisticated general developmental designs and data analysis strategies. It has been emphasized that child psychology principles are perhaps *necessary*, but certainly not *sufficient*, for an integrated developmental psychology. Perhaps only two general principles are necessary to identify a developmental framework: the notions of a system (including structure within the system) and change. Accepting Kessen's (1960) general formulation of developmental characteristics, it is possible to study developmental phenomena at any period in the organism's life span. Although the life-span concept is becoming popular in the developmental literature, developmentalists have attempted to delineate the notions of system and change by employing either specific (stages, ages, levels) or general (development, stabilization, deterioration) guidelines. It is noted again that such guideline terms (including the continual usage of age) may be best defined as generic dependent variables. That is, such terms are basically abstractions or derived variables which are defined by observable referents. It is suggested that guideline terms or generic dependent variables are only markers or abstractions. The principles of system and change are subjected to empirical test only through delineation of physical, psychological, and sociological referents.

Related to the use of derived variables, factors, or constructs in the developmental arena is the idea of a multiple component developmental model. As depicted in Figure 2, numerous model components have been delineated as associated with system, structure and change. These model components must be further delineated, i.e., domain of referents must be specified. Employing a multiple component developmental model, it follows that various combinations of developmental components (e.g., human, sex, race) suggest numerous subdevelopmental disciplines. A word of caution: subdisciplines must be integrated within a general, multidimensional model. The multiple component developmental model does permit such specification of related subdisciplines. Further, levels of design components enable further specification. The general developmental model should promote respect for professional expertise and concern for multidisciplinary approaches. More important, for pedagogical reasons, a developmental model recognizing multiple antecedent-associated variables for system change avoids presenting the student of development with a single construct or theoretical orientation. That is, a multidimensional model, with numerous integrated component delineation attempts, must include all adequate theoretical orientations. Since the utility of the multidimensional model is specification of model components and delineation of constructs (Nunnally's steps *1, 2,* and *3*) it is imperative that a developmentalist of a given theoretical and/or interest orientation recognize the model building attempts of developmentalists with other theoretical and/or interest orientations. And, as many developmentalists of specific period interest (child, adolescent, adult, old age) or general construct interest (geneticists, environmentalists) have recognized the utility of a multidimensional, life-span model, it appears reasonable to assume that disciplines of specific theoretical orientations (cognitive, learning) may do the same. It does appear theoretically feasible, then, that students of behavioral change can participate within a relational schema. How is this developmental—relational system to be accomplished? The answer appears to lie in the understanding, acceptance, and implementation of a developmental-specific research methodology. Developmental-specific methodology is as crucial to developmental construct explication as the life-span approach is to the multidimensional model.

The basic developmental research strategies (cross-sectional and longitudinal methods), represented by Kessen's paradigm ($R = f[A]$), have been criticized as inappropriate for many developmental research problems. Based on earlier corrective attempts in developmental methodology, the multidimensional, uni- and multi-variate designs of Baltes and Schaie emphasize analysis of system-structure change within a life-span model. Such multidimensional, multivariate models expanded in the Primer also emphasize the unconfounding of error components of developmental change. The multiple component developmental model and related univariate and multivariate research strategies should prove useful in developmental construct explication. Such explication should offer basic descriptive data to applied disciplines of behavioral change. With the multitude of social problems facing the applied professional and concerned individual, it is imperative that students and professionals in development offer the applied person principles and applications that have utility. The philosophy or biased point of view advocated in this Primer is that prerequisites of reliable and valid principles are adequate data organization (model) and data collection (design) techniques. It is clear that the "hard" science of the developmentalist dares not criticize the "soft" sciences of the practitioner until the house (models and methods) of the former is in order.

REFERENCES

Aitkin, M. 1971. Statistical theory (behavioral science application). In P.H. Mussen and M. R. Rosenzweig (Eds.), *Annual review of psychology*, vol. 22. Palo Alto: Annual Reviews.
*Anastasi, A. 1958. *Differential psychology* (3rd ed.). New York: Macmillan.
Anderson, J. E. 1954. Methods of child psychology. In L. Carmichael (Ed.), *Manual of child psychology*. New York: Wiley.
Anderson, J. E. (Ed.). 1956a. *Psychological aspects of aging*. Menasha, Wisc.: George Banta.
*Anderson, J. E. 1956b. Research problems in aging. In J. E. Anderson (Ed.), *Psychological aspects of aging*. Menasha, Wisc.: George Banta.
Anderson, T. W. 1958. *An introduction to multivariate statistical analysis*. New York: Wiley.
*Baker, C. T.; Sontag, L. W., and Nelson, V. L. 1958. Individual and group differences in the longitudinal measurement of change in mental ability. *Monographs of the society for research in child development* 23, 11-85.
*Baldwin, A. L. 1960. The study of child behavior and development. In P. H.

NOTE: Starred items in the References indicate works that deal with inherent methodological deficiencies and disadvantages of conventional developmental designs. See footnote, page 31 of this text.

Mussen (Ed.), *Handbook of research methods in child development*. New York: Wiley.
*Baltes, P. B. 1968. Longitudinal and cross-sectional sequences in the study of age and generation effects. *Human Development* 11, 145-171.
Baltes, P. B. 1967. Sequenzmodelle zum Studium von Altersprozessen: Querschnittund Längsschnittsequenzen. In F. Merz (Ed.), *Bericht über den 25. Kongress der Deutschen Gesellschaft für Psychologie in Munster.* Göttingen: Hogrefe.
*Baltes, P. B., and Goulet, L. R. 1970. Status and issues of a life-span developmental psychology. In L. R. Goulet and P. B. Baltes (Eds.), *Life-span developmental psychology: Research and theory*. New York: Academic Press.
Baltes, P. B., and Nesselroade, J. R. 1972. The developmental analysis of individual differences on multiple measures. To appear in J. R. Nesselroade and H. W. Reese (Eds.), *Life-span developmental psychology: Methodological issues*. New York: Academic Press.
*Baltes, P. B., and Nesselroade, J. R. 1970. Multivariate longitudinal and cross-sectional sequences for analyzing ontogenetic and generational charge: A methodological note. *Developmental Psychology* 2, 163-168.
*Baltes, P. B., and Nesselroade, J. R. 1969. Toward a research methodology for the analysis of long-term developmental change: Multivariate longitudinal and cross-sectional sequences. Unpublished manuscript, Department of Psychology, West Virginia University.
Baltes, P. B., and Reinert, G. 1969. Cohort effects in cognitive development of children as revealed by cross-sectional sequences. *Developmental Psychology* 1, 169-177.
*Baumeister, A. A. 1967. Problem of comparative studies of mental retardates and normals. *American Journal of Mental Deficiency* 71, 864-875.
Bayley, N. 1968. Cognition and aging. In K. W. Schaie (Ed.), *Theory and methods of research on aging*. Morgantown, W. Va.: West Virginia University Library.
*Bayley, N. 1963. The life span as a frame of reference in psychological research. *Vita Humana* 6, 125-139.
*Bayley N. 1956. The place of longitudinal studies in research on intellectual factors in aging. In J. E. Anderson (Ed.), *Psychological aspects of aging*. Menasha, Wisc.: George Banta.
Bayley, N., and Oden, M. H. 1955. The maintenance of intellectual ability in gifted adults. *Journal of Gerontology* 10, 91-107.
Bell, R. Q. 1954. An experimental test of the accelerated longitudinal approach. *Child Development* 25, 281-286.
*Bell, R. Q. 1953. Convergence: An accelerated longitudinal approach. *Child Development* 24, 145-152.
Berlyne, D. E. 1966. Discussion: The delimitation of cognitive development. *Monographs of the Society for Research in Child Development* 31, Serial No. 107.
*Bijou, S. W. 1968. Ages, stages, and the naturalization of human development. *American Psychologist* 23, 419-427.

Birren, J. E. (Ed.). 1959a. *Handbook of aging and the individual.* Chicago: University of Chicago Press.
*Birren, J. R. 1959b. Principles of research on aging. In J. E. Birren (Ed.), *Handbook of aging and the individual.* Chicago: University of Chicago Press.
Birren, J. E. 1964. *The psychology of aging.* Englewood Cliffs, N. J.: Prentice-Hall.
*Birren, J. E. 1970. Toward an experimental psychology of aging. *American Psychologist* 25, 124-135.
Bloom, M. 1964. Life span analysis: A theoretical framework for behavioral science research. *Journal of Human Relations* 12, 538-554.
*Block, R. D. 1963. Multivariate analysis of variance of repeated measurements. In C. W. Harris (Ed.), *Problems in measuring change.* Madison: University of Wisconsin Press.
Bock, R. D., and Haggard, E. A. 1968. The use of multivariate analysis of variance in behavioral research. In D. K. Whitla (Ed.), *Handbook of measurement and assessment in behavioral sciences.* Reading, Mass.: Addison-Wesley.
Bonner, J. T. 1963. *Morphogenesis, an essay on development.* New York: Atheneum.
Botwinick, J. 1970. Geropsychology. In P. H. Mussen and M. R. Rosenzweig (Eds.), *Annual review of psychology*, vol. 21. Palo Alto: Annual Reviews.
*Bracht, G. H. and Glass, G. V. 1958. The external validity of experiments. *American Educational Research Journal* 5, 437-474.
Bruner, J. S. 1964. The course of cognitive growth. *American Psychologist* 19, 1-15.
Buhler, C. 1933. Der menschliche Lebenslauf als psychologisches Problem. Leipzig: S. Hirzel. Summarized in E. Frenkel, Studies in biographical psychology. *Character and personality* 5 (1936) 1-34.
Burt, C. 1966. The appropriate uses of factor analysis and analysis of variance. In R. B. Cattell (Ed.), *Handbook of multivariate experimental psychology.* Chicago: Rand McNally.
*Campbell, D. T., and Stanley, J. C. 1963. *Experimental and quasi-experimental designs for research.* Chicago: Rand McNally.
Cattell, R. B. 1966. The data box: Its ordering of total resources in terms of possible relational systems. In R. B. Cattell (Ed.), *Handbook of multivariate experimental psychology.* Chicago: Rand McNally.
Cattell, R. B. 1946. *Description and measurement of personality.* Yonkers-on-Hudson, N. Y.: World Book.
Cattell, R. B. 1952. *Factor analysis.* New York: Harper.
Cole, J. W. L., and Grizzle, J. E. 1966. Applications of multivariate analysis of variance to repeated measurements experiments. *Biometrics* 22, 810-828.
Cooley, W. W., and Lohnes, P. R. 1971. *Multivariate data analysis.* New York: Wiley.
Cooley, W. W., and Lohnes, P. R. 1962. *Multivariate procedures for the behavioral sciences.* New York: Wiley.
Corballis, M. C., and Traub, R. E. 1970. Longitudinal factor analysis. *Psychometrika* 35, 79-98.

Cronbach, L. J. 1957. The two disciplines of scientific psychology. *American Psychologist* 12, 671-684.
*Damon, A. 1956. Discrepancies between findings of longitudinal and cross-sectional studies in adult life: Physique and physiology. *Human Development* 8, 16-22.
Dallett, K. 1969. *Problems of psychology*. New York: Wiley.
Datta, L. 1969. A report on evaluation studies of Project Head Start. Paper presented at the 77th annual American Psychological Convention, Washington, D. C.
*Davies, D. F. 1954. Mortality and morbidity statistics. Limitations of approaches to rates of aging. *Journal of Gerontology* 9, 186-195.
*Dennis, W. 1953. *Age and behavior*. Randolph Field, Texas: U. S. School of Aviation Medicine.
DuBois, P. H. 1965. *An introduction to psychological statistics*. New York: Harper and Row.
Emmerich, W. 1968. Personality development and concepts of structure. *Child Development* 39, 671-690.
Emmerich, W. 1966. Stability and change in early personality development. *Young Children* 21, 233-243.
Erikson, E. 1963. *Childhood and society*. New York: Norton.
*Escalona, S.; Leitch, M.; McFarland, M.; Brody, S.; Heider, C.; and Hollingsworth, I. 1952. Early phases of personality development: A nonnormative study of infant behavior. *Monographs of the Society for Research in Child Development* 17 (1 Serial No. 54).
Flavell, J. H., and Wohlwill, J. F. 1969. Formal and functional aspects of cognitive development. In D. Elkind and J. H. Flavell (Eds.), *Studies in cognitive development: Essays in honor of Jean Piaget*. New York: Oxford University Press.
Fowler, W. 1970. Problems of deprivation and developmental learning. *Merrill-Palmer Quarterly* 16, 141-162.
Freud, S. 1962. *New introductory lectures on psychoanalysis*. New York: Norton.
Freud, S. 1962. *Civilization and its discontents*. New York: Norton.
*Friedrich, D. 1971. Developmental analysis of short-term memory capacity and information encoding strategy. Unpublished Ph. D. dissertation, Psychology Department, Iowa State University.
Friedrich, D.; Fuller, G. B.; and Hawkins, W. F. 1969. Relationship between perception (input) and execution (output). *Perceptual and Motor Skills* 29, 923-934.
Gagné, R. M. 1968. Contributions of learning to human development. *Psychological Review* 75, 177-191.
*Gottman, J. M.; McFall, R. M.; and Barnett, J. T. 1969. Design and analysis of research using time series. *Psychological Bulletin* 72, 299-306.
*Goulet, L. R., and Baltes, P. B. (Eds.). 1970. *Life-span developmental psychology: Research and theory*. New York: Academic Press.
Harman, H. H. 1968. Factor analysis. In D. K. Whitla (Ed.), *Handbook of*

measurement and assessment in behavioral sciences. Reading, Mass.: Addison-Wesley.

Harman, H. H. 1967. *Modern factor analysis.* Chicago: University of Chicago Press.

*Harris, C. W. (Ed.). 1963. *Problems in measuring change.* Madison: University of Wisconsin Press.

Hathaway, S. R. 1965. Personality inventories. In B. B. Wolman (Ed.), *Handbook of clinical psychology.* New York: McGraw-Hill.

Heber, R. F. 1959. A manual on terminology and classification in mental retardation. *American Journal of Mental Deficiency* 64, Monograph Supplement.

Heber, R. F. 1961. A manual on terminology and classification in mental retardation. *American Journal of Mental Deficiency.* Revised Edition, Monograph Supplement.

Hirsch, J. (Ed.). 1967. *Behavior-genetic analysis.* New York: McGraw-Hill.

Horn, J. L. 1965. An empirical comparison of methods for estimating factor scores. *Educational and Psychological Measurement* 25, 313-322.

Horn, J. L. 1970. Organization of data on life-span development of human abilities. In L. R. Goulet and P. B. Baltes (Eds.), *Life-span developmental psychology: Research and theory.* New York: Academic Press.

Horst, P. 1966. An overview of the essentials of multivariate analysis methods. In R. B. Cattell (Ed.), *Handbook of multivariate experimental psychology.* Chicago: Rand McNally.

Horst, P. 1963a. *Matrix algebra for social scientists.* New York: Holt, Rinehart and Winston.

Horst, P. 1963b. Multivariate models for evaluating change. In C. W. Harris (Ed.), *Problems in measuring change.* Madison: University of Wisconsin Press.

Horst, P. 1966. *Psychological measurement and prediction.* Belmont, Calif.: Wadsworth.

Horton, I. F.; Russell, J. S.; and Moore, A. W. 1968. Multivariate-covariance and canonical analysis: A method for selecting the most effective discriminants in a multivariate situation. *Biometrics* 22, 810-828.

Hurlock, E. B. 1959. *Developmental psychology.* New York: McGraw-Hill.

Inhelder, B. 1957. Developmental psychology. In P. R. Farsworth and Q. McNemar (Eds.), *Annual review of psychology.* Palo Alto: Annual Reviews.

Jarvik, L. F., and Falek, A. 1963. Intellectual stability and survival in the aged. *Journal of Gerontology* 18, 173-176.

*Jarvik, L. F.; Kallmann, F. J.; Falek, A.; and Klaber, M. M. 1957. Changing intellectual functions in senescent twins. *Acta Genetica* 7, 421-430.

Jerome, E. A. 1959. Age and learning—experimental studies. In J. E. Birren (Ed.), *A handbook of aging and the individual.* Chicago: University of Chicago Press.

Jones, H. E. 1959. Intelligence and problem solving. In J. E. Birren (Ed.), *Handbook of aging and the individual.* Chicago: University of Chicago Press.

*Jones, H. E. 1958. Problems of method in longitudinal research. *Vita Humana* 1, 93-99.

Jones, L. V. 1966. Analysis of variance in its multivariate developments. In R. B. Cattell (Ed.), *Handbook of multivariate experimental psychology.* Chicago: Rand McNally.

Kagan, J. 1964. American longitudinal research in psychological development. *Child Development* 35, 1-32.

*Kagan, J., and Moss, H. A. 1962. *Birth to maturity: A study in psychological development.* New York: Wiley.

Kallmann, F. J., and Jarvik, L. F. 1959. Individual differences in constitution and genetic background. In J. E. Birren (Ed.), *A handbook of aging and the individual.* Chicago: University of Chicago Press.

*Kamin, L. J. 1957. Differential changes in mental abilities in old age. *Journal of Gerontology* 12, 66-70.

Kendler, T.; Gollin, E.; and Bijou, S. W. 1965. How does the experimental psychologist handle developmental changes that occur with respect to the phenomenon he is interested in? In F. J. Wohlwill (Chr.), Approaches to the experimental-developmental research in child psychology. Symposium presented at the meeting of the Society for Research in Child Development, Minneapolis, Minn.

Kerlinger, F. 1967. *Foundations of Behavioral Research.* New York: Holt, Rinehart and Winston.

Kessen, W. 1966. Questions for a theory of cognitive development. *Monographs of the Society for Research in Child Development* 31 (Whole No. 5), 55-70.

*Kessen, W. 1960. Research design in the study of developmental problems. In P. H. Mussen (Ed.), *Handbook of research methods in child development.* New York: Wiley.

Kirk, R. E. 1968. *Experimental design: Procedures for the behavioral sciences.* Belmont, Calif.: Brooks/Cole.

*Kodlin, D., and Thompson, D. J. 1958. An appraisal of the longitudinal approach to studies in growth and development. *Monographs of the Society for Research in Child Development* 32, No. 67.

Kohlberg, L. 1963. The development of children's orientations toward a moral order. *Vita Humana* 6, 11-33.

*Kuhlen, R. G. 1963. Age and intelligence: The significance of cultural change in longitudinal vs. cross-sectional findings. *Vita Humana* 6, 113-124.

*Kuhlen, R. G. 1952. *The psychology of adolescent development.* New York: Harper.

Looft, W. R. 1972. Socialization and personality throughout the life span: An examination of contemporary psychological approaches. Paper presented at the 3rd West Virginia Conference on Life-span Developmental Psychology: Personality and Socialization, May, 1972.

McClearn, G. E. 1970. Genetic influences on behavior and development. In P. H. Mussen (Ed.), *Manual of child psychology,* vol. 1. New York: Wiley.

McFarland, R. A. 1967. The sensory and perceptual processes in aging. Paper presented at the Conference on Theory and Methods of Research on Aging, West Virginia University.

McGeoch, J. A. 1932. Forgetting and the law of disuse. *Psychological Review* 39, 352-370.
McKusick, V. A. 1964. *Human genetics.* Englewood Cliffs, N. J.: Prentice-Hall.
Marx, M. H. (Ed.). 1963. *Theories in contemporary psychology.* New York: Macmillan.
*Mefferd, R. B., Jr. 1966. Structuring physiological correlates of mental processes and states: The study of biological correlates of mental processes. In R. B. Cattell (Ed.), *Handbook of multivariate experimental psychology.* Chicago: Rand McNally.
Miles, C. C. 1934. Influence of speed and age on intelligence scores of adults. *Journal of General Psychology* 10, 208-210.
Morrison, D. F. 1967. *Multivariate statistical methods.* New York: McGraw-Hill.
Mussen, P. H. (Ed.). 1970. *Manual of child psychology*, vols. 1 and 2. New York: Wiley.
Nagel, E. 1957. Determinism and development. In D. B. Harris (Ed.), *The concept of development.* Minneapolis: University of Minnesota Press.
*Nesselroade, J. R. 1970. Application of multivariate strategies to problems of measuring and structuring long-term change. In L. R. Goulet and P. B. Baltes (Eds.), *Life-span developmental psychology: Research and Theory.* New York: Academic Press.
Nihira, K. 1969. Factorial dimensions of adaptive behavior in adult retardates. *American Journal of Mental Deficiency* 73, 868-878.
Nunnally, J. 1967. *Psychometric theory.* New York: McGraw-Hill.
*Owens, W. A., Jr. 1953. Age and mental abilities: A longitudinal study. *Genetic Psychological Monographs* 48, 3-54.
*Owens, W. A., Jr. 1956. Research on age and mental abilities. In J. E. Anderson (Ed.), *Psychological aspects of aging.* Menasha, Wis.: George Banta.
Piaget, J. 1970. *Piaget's theory.* In P. H. Mussen (Ed.), *Carmichael's manual of child psychology.* New York: Wiley.
Pinard, A., and Laurendeau, M. 1969. "Stage" in Piaget's cognitive-developmental theory: Exegesis of a concept. In D. Elkind, and H. Flavell (Eds.), *Studies in cognitive development: Essays in honor of Jean Piaget.* New York: Oxford University Press. 1969.
Quetelet, A. L. 1835. *Sur l'homme et le dévelopement de ses facultés.* Paris: Bachelier.
Rees, A. H., and Palmer, F. H. 1970. Factors related to change in mental test performance. *Developmental Psychology Monograph* 3 (No. 2, part 2).
Reese, H. W., and Lipsitt, L. P. (Eds.). 1970. *Experimental child psychology.* New York: Academic Press.
Reinert, G. 1970. Comparative factor analytic studies of intelligence throughout the human life span. In L. R. Goulet and P. B. Baltes (Eds.), *Life-span developmental psychology: Research and theory.* New York: Academic Press.
Riegel, K. F. 1968. History as a nomothetic science: Some generalizations from theories and research in developmental psychology. Report No. 74, Center for Human Growth and Development, University of Michigan.

Riegel, K. R.; Riegel, R. M.; and Meyer, G. 1967a. A study of drop-out rates in longitudinal research on aging and the prediction of death. *Journal of Personality and Social Psychology* 5, 324-348.

Riegel, K. F.; Riegel, R. M.; and Meyer, G. 1967b. Sociopsychological factors of aging: A cohort-sequential analysis. *Human Development* 10, 27-56.

Riley, M. W., and Foner, A. (Eds.). 1968. *Aging and society,* vol. 1, New York: Russell Sage Foundation.

Roa, M. N., and Roa, C. R. 1966. Methods for determining norms and growth rates: A study amongst Indian school-going boys. *Gerontologia* 12, 200-216.

Rosler, H. D. 1966. Acceleration and intelligence capacity in adults (abstract). *Ber. 18, Intern. Kongr. Psychol.* Moskau, 3, 54.

Rummel, R. J. 1970. *Applied factor analysis.* Evanston: Northwestern University Press.

*Sanderson, R. E., and Inglis, J. 1961. Learning and mortality in elderly psychiatric patients. *Journal of Gerontology* 16, 375-376.

*Schaie, K. W. 1965. A general model for the study of developmental problems. *Psychological Bulletin* 64, 92-107.

*Schaie, K. W. 1970. A reinterpretation of age related changes in cognitive structure and functioning. In L. R. Goulet and P. B. Baltes (Eds.), *Life-span developmental psychology: Research and theory.* New York: Academic Press.

*Schaie, K. W. 1967. Age changes and age differences. *The Gerontologist* 7, 128-132.

*Schaie, K. W. 1959. Cross-sectional methods in the study of psychological aspects of aging. *Journal of Gerontology* 14, 208-215.

Schaie, K. W. 1958. Rigidity-flexibility and intelligence: A cross-sectional study of the adult life-span from 20 to 70. *Psychological Monographs* 72 (462, Whole No. 9).

*Schaie, K. W., and Strother, C. R. 1968a.The cross-sequential study of age changes in cognitive behavior. *Psychological Bulletin* 70, 671-680.

*Schaie, K. W., and Strother, C. R. 1968b. The effects of time and cohort differences on the interpretation of age changes in cognitive behavior. *Multivariate Behavioral Research* 3, 259-293.

Scott, J. P. 1962. Critical periods in behavioral development. *Science* 138, 949-958.

Sinnott, E. W.; Dunn, L. C.; and Dobzhansky, T. 1958. *Principles of genetics.* New York: McGraw-Hill.

*Smith, N. C., Jr. 1970. Replication studies: A neglected aspect of psychological research. *American Psychologist* 25, 970-975.

*Solomon, R. L., and Lessac, M. S. 1968. A control group design for experimental studies of developmental processes. *Psychological Bulletin* 70, 145-150.

*Stone, A. A., and Onque, G. C. 1959. *Longitudinal studies of child personality.* Cambridge: Harvard University Press.

Talland, C. A. (Ed.). 1968. *Human aging and behavior: Recent advances in research and theory.* New York: Academic Press.

Tatsuoka, M. M. 1971. *Multivariate analysis: Techniques for educational and psychological research.* New York: Wiley.
*Thomas, A.; Chess, S.; Birch, H. G.; Hertsizk, M.; and Korn, S. 1963. *Behavioral individuality in early childhood.* New York: New York University Press.
Van Den Daele, L. D. 1969. Qualitative models in developmental analysis. *Developmental Psychology* 1, 303-334.
Wapner, S. 1964. Some aspects of a research program based on an organismic-developmental approach to cognition: Experiments and theory. *Journal of the American Academy of Child Psychiatry* 3, 193-230.
Welford, A. T. 1964. *Vieillissement et aptitudes humaines.* Paris: Presses Universitaires de France.
*Welford, A. T. 1961. Methode longitudinale et transversale dans les recherches sur le vieillissement. In Colloques Internationaux du Centre de la Recherche Scientifique (Ed.), *Le vieillissement des fonctions psychologiques et psychophysiologiques.* Paris: Centre National.
Werner, H. 1948. *Comparative psychology of mental development.* Chicago: Follett.
Werner, H. 1957. The concept of development from a comparative and organismic point of view. In D. Harris (Ed.), *The concept of development: An issue in the study of human behavior.* Minneapolis: University of Minnesota Press.
Windle, C. 1954. Test-retest effect on personality questionnaires. *Educational and Psychological Measurement* 14, 617-633.
Winer, B. J. *Statistical principles in experimental design.* New York: McGraw-Hill, 1962.
*Wohlwill, F. J. (Chm.). 1965. Approaches to experimental-developmental research in child psychology. Symposium presented at the meeting of the Society for Research in Child Development, Minneapolis, Minn.
*Wohlwill, J. F. 1969. Methodology and research strategy in the study of developmental change. *Educational Testing Service Research Memorandum.*
*Wohlwill, J. F. 1970a. Methodology and research strategy in the study of developmental change. In L. R. Goulet and P. B. Baltes (Eds.), *Life-span developmental psychology: Research and theory.* New York: Academic Press.
*Wohlwill, J. F. 1970b. The age variable in psychological research. *Psychological Review* 77, 49-64.
Wolins, L. 1969. Some computational, methodological, and theoretical considerations relevant to summarizing psychological data. Unpublished manuscript, Psychology Department, Iowa State University.
*Woodruff, D. S., and Birren, J. E. 1972. Age changes and cohort differences in personality. *Developmental Psychology* 6, 252-259.
Yerkes, R. M. 1913. Comparative psychology: A question of definitions. *Journal of Philosophical Psychology and Scientific Methods* 10, 580-582.
Zigler, E. 1963. Metatheoretical issues in developmental psychology. In N. H. Marx (Ed.), *Theories in contemporary psychology.* New York: Macmillan.

SUBJECT INDEX

Age, 7, 39
  difference, 51
  interacting with particular population, 33
  interacting with environmental change, 34
  interacting with particular population and environmental change, 35
Aging research, 17
Assortative mating, 44
Basic data matrix, 81
  and developmental research, 84
Basic data relational system, 78
Bifactorial developmental model, 70
Bilaterally multivariate designs, 101
Change, 13
Change over time, 1, 7, 11
Classical developmental designs, 19
  contradictions of, 31, 32
  problems of, 25
Cognitive adaptation, 16, 17
Cohort, 35, 40
  difference, 51
  sequential method, 47, 56
Comparative developmental psychology, 41
Comparative factor analysis, 80, 81
Completely randomized design, 32
Consolidation, 2
Construct, 9
Construct delineation, 105
  and developmental research, 106
Correlational techniques, 86
Criterion, 21
  attribute, 84
Cross-sectional design, 19
Cross-sectional difference, 51
Cross-sectional sequence, 74
Cross-sequential method, 47, 62
Culture, 41
Cumulative learning model, 4, 14
Developmental construct explication, 16
Developmental design components, 13, 40

Developmental framework, 1
Dimensions for classifying developmental approaches, 3
Dimensions of developmental models, 2
Elementary points of development, 11
Equilibration, 2
Experimental mortality, 36
Factor, 86
  loading pattern matrix, 86
  and developmental research, 97
  scores, 98
  and developmental research, 99
Five-dimensional model, 41
General developmental model, 47, 78
Generation effects, 37
Generic dependent variable, 15
Genetic–environment interaction, 14, 44
Hierarchization, 2
Independent measurements, 71
Individual identity, 30
Integration, 2
Inter-individual variation, 29
Intervening constructs, 9
Intra-individual variation, 30
Invariant loading patterns, stable factor scores, 100
  fluctuant factor scores, 100
Laws of behavioral change, 8
Learning models, 10
Life-span model, 17, 18
Longitudinal design, 19, 23
  practical problems of, 30
Longitudinal difference, 51
Longitudinal program, 24, 25
Longitudinal sequence, 74
Matrix operations, 79
Mental age, 15
Modes of representation, 2
Multidimensional model, 42, 78
Multivariate analysis of variance, 80, 101
  and developmental research, 103
Multivariate data collection designs: dependent variables, 77

Multivariate data collection designs: sequential strategies, 45
Noninvariant loading patterns, stable factor scores, 100
 fluctuant factor scores, 100
Phenotype, 14
Physiological maturation, 14
Predictor attributes, 84
Pre-experimental designs, 27
Qualitative change, 2, 3
Quantitative change, 2, 3
Repeated measurements, 71
Repeated measures design, 59, 65
Selective dropout, 36
 sampling, 35
 survival, 35
Species, 41
Stages of cognitive development, 2, 14
Static models, 10, 18
Structure, 13
Structuring, 2
Subdevelopmental disciplines, 43
Summary labels, 14
Supermatrix, 84
System, 13
Testing effects, 36
Three dimensional model, 40, 45, 67
Time difference, 51
Time-lag design, 45
Time-lag difference, 51
Time of measurement, 40
Time-sequential method, 47, 49
Unidimensional formula, 26, 31, 40
Unilaterally multivariate designs, 101
Univariate analysis, 77
Validity, internal, 27
 external, 27
 population, 28
 ecological, 28
Variable temporal patterning, 30
Variable relationship patterning, 30
Variance components, 31, 53
Vector, 103

NAME INDEX

Aitkin, M., 101, 102
Anastasi, A., 36, 37, 45
Anderson, J., 36, 102
Baker, C., 35, 36
Baltes, P., 19, 25, 27, 29, 30, 31, 35, 37, 38, 39, 41, 43, 45, 60, 61, 67, 70, 71, 72, 74, 75, 76, 77, 78, 79, 80, 81, 97, 98, 99, 100, 101, 109
Barnett, J., 31
Baumeister, A., 15
Bayley, N., 29, 37
Bell, R., 45
Berlyne, D., 8, 9
Bijou, S., 4, 11, 14, 15
Birren, J., 36, 37, 45, 77
Bock, R., 102
Bonner, J., 6
Botwinick, J., 31
Bracht, G., 28
Bruner, J., 2, 14
Burt, C., 80, 102
Campbell, D., 19, 27, 36, 37, 39
Cattell, R., 5, 78, 79, 80, 86, 87, 88, 89, 101, 104, 105
Chess, S., 30
Cole, J., 102
Cooley, W., 102
Corballis, M., 80
Cronbach, L., 105
Damon, A., 36, 37, 46
Dobzhansky, T., 6
BuBois, P., 53, 54
Dunn, L., 6
Emmerich, W., 5, 6
Erikson, E., 6, 7
Falek, A., 36
Flavell, J., 2
Fowler, W., 14
Freud, S., 5, 7
Friedrich, D., 11, 21, 22
Fuller, G., 21, 22
Gagne, R., 4, 14

Glass, G., 28
Gottman, J., 31
Goulet, L., 29, 31, 45
Grizzle, J., 102
Haggard, E., 102
Harman, H., 91, 92, 98
Harris, C., 31
Hathaway, S., 80
Hawkins, W., 21, 22
Heber, R., 21
Horn, J., 80, 98
Horst, P., 80, 81, 82, 91
Horton, I., 78, 102
Inhelder, B., 17
Jarvik, L., 36, 46
Jerome, E., 37
Jones, L., 101, 102
Kagan, J., 24, 25
Kallmann, F., 46
Kerlinger, F., 86
Kessen, W., 6, 17, 26, 27, 31, 33, 34, 35, 39, 40, 60, 61, 68, 107, 108
Kirk, R., 53, 59, 65
Kodlin, D., 35, 36
Kohlberg, L., 7
Korn, S., 30
Kuhlen, R., 36, 37
Laurendeau, M., 3
Lessac, M., 31
Lipsitt, L., 17
Lohnes, P., 102
Looft, W., 3, 4, 5, 7, 8
Marx, M., 9
McFall, R., 31
McGeoch, J., 11
Meyer, G., 36, 77
Miles, C., 36
Moore, A., 78, 102
Morrison, D., 102
Mussen, P., 17
Nagel, E., 13
Nelson, V., 35, 36

Nesselroade, J., 31, 39, 41, 43, 45, 71, 76, 77, 78, 79, 80, 81, 86, 89, 97, 98, 99, 100, 101, 105
Nihira, K., 93, 95, 97
Nunnally, J., 80, 86, 87, 88, 89, 91, 98, 105, 106, 107, 108
Owens, W., 36
Palmer, F., 79
Piaget, J., 2, 3, 4, 5, 6, 14, 15, 16
Pinard, A., 3
Quetelet, A., 18
Rees, A., 79
Reese, H., 17, 79
Reinert, G., 77, 80
Riegel, K., 13, 14, 15, 36, 77
Riegel, R., 36, 77
Rosler, H., 37
Rummel, R., 98
Russell, J., 76, 102
Schaie, K., 29, 31, 37, 39, 40, 41, 45, 46, 47, 48, 49, 50, 51, 52, 53, 55, 56, 57, 58, 59, 61, 62, 63, 64, 65, 66, 67, 68, 69, 70, 71, 74, 76, 77, 78, 79, 97, 98, 109
Scott, J., 6
Sinnott, E., 6
Solomon, R., 31
Sontag, L., 35, 36
Stanley, J., 19, 27, 36, 37, 39
Strother, C., 46, 70, 77
Tatsuoka, M., 102, 103
Thomas, A., 30
Thompson, D., 35, 36
Traub, R., 80
Van den Daele, L., 5, 6, 15, 16, 17
Wapner, S., 41, 45
Welford, A., 36, 37, 45
Werner, H., 14, 17, 41, 78
Windle, C., 36
Winer, B., 60
Wohlwill, J., 2, 19, 30, 31, 45, 46, 49, 60, 61, 67, 76, 77
Woodruff, D., 77
Yerkes, R., 41, 78